# LOVE GOD
# HEAL EARTH

**DATE DUE**

# LOVE GOD
# HEAL EARTH

The Rev. Canon Sally G. Bingham

st. lynn's
*press*

PITTSBURGH

Love God, Heal Earth
21 Leading Religious Voices Speak Out on
Our Sacred Duty to Protect the Environment

ISBN-13: 978-0-9800288-3-6

Library of Congress Control Number: 2008933291
CIP information available upon request

First Edition, 2009

St. Lynn's Press . POB 18680 . Pittsburgh, PA 15236
412.466.0790 . www.stlynnspress.com

Typesetting—Holly Wensel, Network Printing Services
Cover design—Jeff Nicoll
Editors—Catherine Dees, Abby Dees

Note: The editors have honored the individual contributors' preferences for capitalizing or not capitalizing the words "earth," "creation," "creator" and "evangelical."

Printed in the United States of America
on recycled paper

This title and all of St. Lynn's Press books may be purchased for educational, business, or sales promotional use. For information please write:

Special Markets Department . St. Lynn's Press
POB 18680 . Pittsburgh, PA 15236

10 9 8 7 6 5 4 3 2 1

for Lock, Stephen and Sarah, my lifelines

# Table of Contents

# Introduction

❧

Now faith is the assurance of things hoped for,
the conviction of things not seen.

(Hebrews 11:1)

The bad news first: The climate is changing. The good news: So are people of faith.

There is an awakening to global warming that I could only dream about ten years ago. It started with a handful of religious leaders (me included) pleading the Earth's case from the pulpit. Now, amazingly, the health of the Earth and its inhabitants has become a priority issue for mainstream religion. Perhaps we are even starting to open our collective consciousness to the possibility that we are part of something greater than ourselves and we have a responsibility for stewardship, not only for each other, but for that greater "something."

How can I say this with such optimism, when our human behavior has brought us to the brink of our own destruction? I say it because my faith provides and inspires hope. Those two things, faith and hope, have led my ministry. But there is more than that: The change on the horizon is the culmination of a collective effort on the part of mainstream religious leaders to address a long over-due responsibility – care for Creation.

I'll be the first to say that the religious environmental movement has been late in forming. Despite the prescient wisdom of some who came before, like St. Francis and before him St. Augustine, we haven't had much time to compare notes or agree on a global strategy for interfaith action. This new call to put faith into action is only a few years old.

## THE LEARNING YEARS

Here is how it started for me. In the early 1990s, the religious-eco-justice movement was still in an embryonic stage. I was in seminary when a fellow student, Ben Webb, and I started sharing our thoughts about this. In 1994, after Ben had written up the concept of how we could "deepen the connection between ecology and faith," we founded The Regeneration Project (TRP) – and together set out to inform local congregations that if you sit in a pew and profess a love for God and Creation then you were responsible for the well-being of Creation. We were ahead of the curve, and few people understood what we were trying to do; even fewer were willing to fund us. Ben (now The Rev. Ben Webb) had a family to support and moved to Iowa, while I went back to school fulltime, and on to ordination as a Priest in the Diocese of California.

In 1996, I met Steve MacAusland, an Episcopal layperson living in Massachusetts. We were both attending a meeting of the national Episcopal Church Ecological Network. Bored with continuous rhetoric and passionately interested in getting something done, we began making a plan, focusing on climate change. His vision and our combined imaginations created Episcopal Power and Light and made it the first and primary program under The Regeneration Project. Coincidentally (or spirit driven), both California where I live and Massachusetts where he lived had just deregulated their electrical industries, allowing consumers for the first time to choose their utility and source for their electricity. This was the perfect opportunity to inform people of faith about the negative impact of traditional sources of energy.

For the next three years Steve and I went parish by parish, asking both California and Massachusetts churches to switch their electricity provider from the local utility to a green provider. (Steve divided his time between coasts, but since it was an easier process in California than in Massachusetts, California became the lead model for what was to become Interfaith Power and Light. Steve eventually stayed in Massachusetts to be at the helm of the MA IPL.)

Once we had proclaimed parishioners "sinners" for buying power from dirty-burning coal plants that were located mostly in poor communities, they took our advice and switched from the local utility to a clean green provider. In three years' time we had 60 parishes in California who were customers, buying power generated 100% by wind. The deal we struck with the energy provider, Green Mountain, was a first of its kind. Episcopal Power and Light served as a promoter of Green Mountain, which in turn made a donation to the congregations for every parishioner who signed up. It was a win-win. We were getting parishes and parishioners to switch to clean energy, this was building Green Mountain's business and our churches were doing the right thing. Everyone was pleased.

Then in 2000, the state of California went through the now famous "energy crisis," which exposed serious flaws in the deregulation system; and Green Mountain, along with the other clean energy providers, left the state for fear of going bankrupt. Our Episcopal churches that were customers of Green Mountain were disgruntled, to say the least, and I had to recover my credibility — and the credibility of the cause. I decided to forge ahead with faith.

Beyond the appealing goal of helping churches save money by doing the right thing, the issue was still climate change and saving the planet by cutting carbon emissions, a major contributor to the warming of our planet. Even without buying green energy, I knew that we could continue to reduce carbon emissions by focusing on two things: energy efficiency and conservation. And so, thinking big, and with some funding from a Southern California foundation, I hired a consultant. I could see that the energy crisis had actually presented us with an opportunity. The whole state was being asked to conserve energy to avoid the rolling blackouts that had begun to plague our electricity grid. Instead of focusing exclusively on green energy, we could offer a suite of clean energy choices to congregations, starting with conservation. And by expanding beyond the 450 Episcopal churches in California to congregations of all faiths, we could reach a much greater audience. But I would need partners. So we called a meeting in Oakland with the California Council of Churches, the Southern California Ecumenical Council, the Northern California Inter-religious Conference, and the Coalition on the Environment and Jewish Life. All of us together decided that day to become Interfaith Power and Light.

## How We Became a Movement
## (with a few bumps along the way)

We set out to have every house of worship in California cut their emissions. The ministry was unique. We were now approaching the broader religious community that had to be convinced about the validity of considering energy use for *theological* reasons. Of course, saving Creation is central to most faiths, but until the middle to late 1990s few if any religious leaders so much as mentioned it. Some were suspicious and went so far as to say that taking care of the environment was a political issue and didn't belong in the church. There was resistance on many fronts. Besides being a political issue, environmental concerns were seen by some as way too liberal for many congregations. "Tree huggers" we were called and accused of liking trees more than people. One clergy person said to me "I am not an issue person." My response was, "This isn't an issue, this is life and death." I was not popular, but I carried on.

Gradually, word of Interfaith Power and Light (IPL) spread and was picked up in the media, causing a large charitable foundation to seek us out and offer to help us hire a national campaign manager and take our California model into other states. We accepted and started almost immediately in Massachusetts. In the next few months, The Rev. Woody Bartlett in Georgia invited me down to help launch a program there. There was interest from Minnesota, New York, New Mexico and Connecticut. They were some of the early ones.

An important IPL (though not called that at the time) began before we were even aware of each other. I had never heard of Wyandott, a quiet town in Michigan where The Rev. Charles

Morris had already put solar panels and a small wind turbine on the roof of the rectory of his Catholic church, St. Elizabeth, in an attempt to show that clean energy works and that he could have electrical power even if the grid went down. Coincidently, my college-age son was attending Michigan State, and when I went to parents weekend, I contacted Charles. We became friends and colleagues almost instantly. Charles has led one of our most important IPL programs, Shop IPL (started by Michigan IPL and adopted for all state IPLs to use). The members can buy energy efficient appliances below cost and have them delivered to the door of the congregations. This was done in partnership with the Environmental Protection Agency and their Energy Star® for Congregations program.

In the eight years between 2001 and now, we have grown from two state programs to 27, and one in the Greater Washington DC area. These 28 programs are now the leading faith community advocates for climate protection in America. The people at the helms are, in some cases, volunteers passionately committed to helping the planet survive human destructive behavior. Over half are paid staff with their own independent 501(c)(3) status; some much larger than others, but all working on a religious response to global warming. The story is amazing and the people involved are equally amazing. From struggling to be taken as a moral responsibility just a few years ago, this global warming ministry has become a national phenomenon. We are on the edge of something great and we know we are doing the right thing. Not to sound flip about this, most of us would say that we are being led by the Spirit. The success of The Regeneration Project's Interfaith Power and Light Campaign has overwhelmed the people involved. We must be doing something right and it may well be that we happen to be in the right place at the right time. My own motivation comes from saying "yes" more often than not. Yes to God and yes to stretching my imagination. Our national office has a staff of seven. We are coordinating a national movement that grows bigger and more influential daily. I live in wonder of the success.

## THE MORAL IMPERATIVE

In the last five years and particularly in the last three, many things have happened that have caused the skeptics in the US to slowly but surely succumb to the truth. There is consensus in the scientific community (see www.ipcc.ch) with the Intergovernmental Panel on Climate Change, a group of 2500 scientist from 55 countries agreeing that humans are causing most of the problem. There is the film An Inconvenient Truth, which we distributed to over 4000 congregations in our network and screened to a half a million people. The droughts in the West, the floods in the middle of the country, tornados at the wrong time of year and the increasing death rate due to heat waves that last longer than ever before have made climate change a fact and not a theory. The severity of Katrina and the profound evidence that poor and vulnerable communities are targets for disaster has brought climate change to the faith community as a matter of social justice, something religion has historically addressed.

People of faith are now hearing about climate change from the media, but more importantly, they are hearing it preached from the pulpit, spoken in the mosques and synagogues from a moral perspective. The subject is deeply moral and religious. How we respond will dictate the future for generations to come. People living today will have to decide if we want our legacy to be one of slash and burn or one of healing and reconciliation. Our response will show whether or not we love our neighbors (neighbors near and far, next generation neighbors) – and in many ways it will show our love for God and God's Creation.

If we are moral beings, which I believe we are, and if we want to do the right thing, which I believe we do, then we will turn this warming trend around. We are creative, intelligent people with a strong will to protect ourselves and our children. Once we know the seriousness of the threat, and I believe we are at that point, we will start to solve the problem. Speaking from a preachy perspective, I believe that people of faith cannot stand by and let Creation be destroyed. We have a responsibility to protect it. We have dominion, for God's sake. Dominion isn't exploit and plunder, dominion is care, compassion and concern. The kind of dominion that God has over us and is described in one word – LOVE. It is about taking care of what has been given for us to use, but not abuse.

## A Defining Moment, and None Too Soon

My purpose for this book is not to write about the destruction we see all around us or give yet more statistics on how many coral reefs have died, numbers of species going extinct, high rates of cancer due to pollution, etc, but rather to provide the hope we need to persevere and keep on looking for solutions. I, and the 20 others whose words appear here, want our readers to know that we are moving toward the change that needs to be made, and that religion is playing an important role. When you read through these chapters in *Love God, Heal Earth*, you will get a sense of how this message is professed to the different traditions they represent. It is a snapshot of a moment in human history – Earth history – when the future hung in the balance and communities of faith came together out of love for Creation.

We hope you will be struck by the knowledge that there are religious leaders doing wonderful, creative work to heal Earth from further destruction. There are persistent and profound themes here, ones that to me, point to the great change of consciousness I have witnessed in my own ministry. Perhaps the most enduring concept within these pages is that the environment is an issue of compassion, not politics. Often, especially in America, religious leaders avoid the taint of politics in the pulpit. The reasons for this range from the belief that the relative pettiness and secular nature of politics distracts us from our greater spiritual quest...to the fear of alienating our diverse congregations...to nervousness that we'll run afoul of the IRS and its First Amendment proscriptions (Richard Cizik writes also of the intractability of an old model of Christian worship that focuses on the spiritual to the exclusion of the material world; this may be an issue within other faiths as well).

In my Judeo-Christian tradition, we have the commandments to love God and to love thy neighbor as thyself. Some religious traditions say it differently, but we all have more or less the same message: Muslims talk about balance and wholeness (Mohamad Chakaki writes of the Muslim concept of Fitra, the knowledge of oneness, as I roughly read it), Buddhists talk about interconnectedness ("our inextricable connection to the universe," as Linda Cutts describes it). In short, we are connected to each other. We belong to one another and we have a responsibility to one another. It is a direct violation of our faiths to stand by and let our home, our neighbor's home, the gift of the Creator, perish. This is the realm of religion, no doubt about it. In fact, religion has a special duty here, as Professor Mary Evelyn Tucker writes, because it has "the ability to change from within and to spark change from without."

I hope you will find in the following pages examples that you can incorporate into your own ministry or worship. More than this, I hope that these words will nourish your soul and your own relationship with Creation. Join together with us and a leader in your faith who is involved with an Interfaith Power and Light ministry, or another ministry that suits your personal integrity. Whatever you take away from these chapters, you can rest assured that the people and ministries presented here are working for you and for the survival of the human species. Thomas Berry, a well-known theologian and social historian who is mentioned more than once in this book, was heard asking the question, "Is the human race sustainable?" I think the answer is, "Yes, but..." We will need to become conscious of our behavior, follow our faith's call to be stewards of Creation and believe in the power of the Spirit to move us toward a healthy planet. The goal is simple, the means are going to involve us all.

Please feel free to contact any of the contributors to *Love God, Heal Earth*. We will be happy to hear from you.

Sally Bingham
January, 2009
San Francisco

THE REV. RICHARD CIZIK

FORMER VICE-PRESIDENT FOR GOVERNMENTAL AFFAIRS

NATIONAL ASSOCIATION OF EVANGELICALS

# What If?

"The good news is that the climate deny-ers, aided and abetted by the religious right, are losing all the arguments on all counts – theology, politics and science. Climate change is not 'the devil's diversion,' as the late Reverend Jerry Falwell admonished his congregation."

W hat if there were a planet so perfectly balanced that millions of species thrived in realms of water, land and air? What if a single species became so powerful that it began to change the very nature of the planet itself? It is happening now, and only one species has the power to stop it: Ours.

The world is getting warmer. This past summer I visited what could be called our "early warming system" for North America, an island village named Shishmaref, located off the coast of Alaska in the Bering Sea. The native tribe of Inupiks are already experiencing a devastating blow: a sea-level rise that is forcing them from their homes of the last 400 years. The impoverished residents of the coastal megacities in the Third World will soon face a similar fate. For them, it's not a matter of halting climate change — it's too late for that; learning to adapt is the challenge.

Those species that do adapt, survive. Those that don't, according to Professor Bob Doppelt, a climatologist and systems analyst at the University of Oregon, go extinct. Human beings have a greater capacity to adapt, but won't necessarily do so. To Professor Doppelt's systems-focused mind, climate change has the capacity to "determine the winners and losers." Climate change will even determine the fate of religious movements and political parties.

Why hasn't the faith community been more vocal? Long ago, the Christian faith community sacrificed its voice on the environment. The early Church fathers substituted a platonic vision that emphasized the spiritual over the material for proper stewardship of Creation. Reformers in the 17th and 18th centuries viewed the earth as nothing more than a stage for the contest over man's soul. And in more recent decades, religious believers were more than willing to turn over their duties from God to the State. Nowadays, the typical believer who has been entrusted with stewardship duties has given that role over to the government. This concept of "fiduciary ownership" is understandable, and even justifiable, but it would seem to call for an engagement with the political world to assure that that ownership is exercised wisely.

But speaking out can be hazardous. I've had leaders of the religious right accuse me of being "anti-capitalist and having an underlying hatred for America" simply for speaking out on behalf of creation care. (James Dobson's "Focus on the Family" broadcast, May 19, 2006)

What's behind this?

Some of it can be attribute to the following attitudes:

- Environmentalists are disdained as "leftists,"
- Mainstream science is distrusted on account of evolution and Darwin,
- Mainstream media is viewed as "hyping" stories about the environment, thus these stories are rejected as scaremongering
- Free-market economics is distrustful of governmental solutions, and
- The tenet that mankind shall have dominion over the earth means that we can do whatever we want with it.

And you can add one more ingredient to this noxious brew: The environment is not divided by national or political boundaries, but is a global entity. Thus it is potentially beyond personal perception and realistically foreseeable political will. At least that's how some have seen the situation.

"It's the devil's diversion," said the late preacher Jerry Falwell in a 2007 sermon about global warming. In other words, it diverts Christians from their rightful calling to preach the Gospel. He added that it was only those blue-state Democrats, UN types, "liberal clergymen, and some evangelicals who are uninformed" that take climate change seriously. I was surely among those "misinformed" evangelicals, since a video clip of his comments was broadcast as part of CNN's "God's Christian Warriors," which included a segment on my activities to broaden the agenda of evangelicals to include creation care.

Who's right? Well, if evangelicals took their advice from certain leaders within fundamentalist Christianity, there was little prospect (and I wish I'd been proven wrong) that the presidential election of 2008 would see a contest about the environment – unlike Britain, where both political parties vie to become the "greenest."

Despite all the attention to the run-up in gas prices, and whether oil companies are to blame, one statistic is worth mentioning: According to reliable sources, during the primary debates in the 2008 election campaign, over 2,000 questions were asked of all the candidates, but only three times were the candidates asked about climate change. That is an amazingly paltry number, given the seriousness of the climate crisis. So, for those who believe that "the media" is liberal and environmentally sensitive, think again.

But the good news is that evangelicals are not listening to the voices of unreason or anti-scientific philosophy. For a long time the segment of the evangelical community that is fundamentalist has had the biggest megaphone, but that loud voice is now being challenged.

The 100-member Board of Directors of the National Association of Evangelicals resisted the call by 25 leaders of the conservative movement to silence my advocacy as too "divisive." The board even went on record in March 2007 to unanimously endorse (again) the document, "For the Health of the Nation: An Evangelical Call to Civic Responsibility," which outlines creation care as a biblical duty. As for my being "divisive," I can only respond by noting that this was the same charge used in my father's generation against action on civil rights.

Over 100 national leaders from the largest ministries in America, including World Vision, The Salvation Army, megachurch pastors such as Rick Warren of Saddleback Church, not to mention all of the top leaders of the National Association of Evangelicals (NAE), such as President Leith Anderson, have signed the "Evangelical Climate Initiative." That 2006 document states the caring for our environment is a biblical duty and that the government has a role to play in addressing climate change — starting now.

Moreover, recent surveys by the Ellison Research Group, Inc., reveal that 75% of evangelicals believe that climate change is real and will impact their lives. Even more, 84%, believe that the Congress should pass a mandatory limit on greenhouse gas emissions, an idea reflected in the "Climate Security Act," recently passed out of a Senate Environment Subcommittee, albeit along nearly partisan lines. Democrats supported the bill and most Republicans opposed it. This could turn out to be a monumental political mistake, similar to Republican opposition to civil rights in the 1960's.

Evangelicals are becoming the "go to" religious community on the environment, despite opposition by high profile leaders such as James Dobson of Focus On The Family, and others. While the fundamentalist wing still evidences anti-intellectual tendencies, the broader movement is rapidly shedding itself of old anti-scientific attitudes and speaking out for creation stewardship.

According to a 2006 Baylor University Survey, one hundred million Americans call themselves evangelicals, and make up from 40 to 50 percent of the conservative base of the GOP. Up until now, this community has given President Bush and his party the equivalent of a "pass" on global warming. Instead, they've supported "voluntary" measures to (in the words of Vice President Cheney) "be virtuous" with regard to environmental policy. And they've allowed the GOP to get away with this business-as-usual approach for too long.

But as the evangelical community embraces creation care, the danger for the Republicans is enormous. If the evangelicals see the Grand Old Party as "old guard" and unable to address the major national issues facing the nation, they could desert in droves. There's a saying, "As evangelicalism goes, so goes the West." It would only take a small percentage of the voting adult evangelicals – one quarter of the voting public – to turn the outcome of some elections.

Thus far, the environment has never been a top voting priority, but evangelicals could change that dismal reality. My prediction is that if Congress doesn't act to cut greenhouse gas emissions and implement a free-market mechanism to bring industry and the private sector on board, the political party that's responsible for holding up environmental action will suffer in the long run.

The good news is that the climate deny-ers, aided and abetted by the religious right, are losing all the arguments on all counts – theology, politics and science. Climate change is not "the devil's diversion," as the late Reverend Jerry Falwell admonished his congregation that day at Thomas Road Baptist Church in Lynchburg, Virginia. It may be God's way to get our attention, a love letter of sorts from the Creator of the Universe alerting us that we are living in selfish sin – how else can you describe a situation in which we in the United States, representing 4.5% of the world's population, contribute 25% of the world's greenhouse gas emissions? We need to repent. And unless we do come to experience this metanoia and change the very way we live, we are all in peril.

Are the opponents of the "new evangelicals," (as Mark Opinsky of the Orlando Sentinel refers to those of us who are advocating for a broader engagement with the world on issues such as poverty, genocide and the environment) all that concerned about the nation's top evangelicals succumbing to paganism or earth worship? Not likely.

Their concern is more about politics than theology. It comes down to this: If evangelicals accept the legitimacy of the environment as a public-policy priority, they may be less inclined to vote Republican.

In the past, global warming has been a significant wedge issue. Those who haven fallen into the category of "climate critics" have also been interested in preserving the relationship between big business (particularly big oil) and evangelical conservatives – the two wings of the Republican Party. Critics refer to this as an "unholy alliance" that gives lip service to evangelical social issues while securing billions in tax cuts and subsidies to corporate elites. Some even refer to this in terms of "conspiracy theories." Well, it's not a secret conspiracy. It's right out in the open. In my judgment, it reveals a misplaced allegiance by my fellow conservatives. It would appear that they care more about the welfare of the Republican Party than they do the Kingdom of God. If that's not the case, they should say so.

And what of those evangelicals who still believe that the earth is bound for destruction and unworthy of their concern? This is the idea that there's no logic in rearranging the deck chairs on the Titanic. A small percentage sincerely believes this, but their numbers are declining. During a recent speaking engagement at Hardin-Simmons University chapel service, a student interrupted me to ask, "If we know the world will end in fire anyway, what does it matter?" The answer, of course, is that the entire teaching of the Bible from Genesis ("Care and protect it [the creation]") to Revelations ("I will destroy those who destroy the earth") teaches our biblical duty to exercise stewardship over the creation. (Genesis 2:15 and Revelation 11:18)

But generally, in all of my travels over the past few years, visiting campuses and churches, seldom does "arm-chair Armageddonism," as I refer to it, actually arise. creation care is a theology of earth stewardship which comes straight from the Word of God. Passages, for example, such as Matthew 6:20 ("[S]tore up for yourselves treasures in heaven, where moth and rust do not destroy....") require that we strive to bring the sustainable values of heaven to earth. That's surely a reasonable application of the Lord's Prayer in which Jesus urges his followers to seek "thy kingdom come on earth as it is in heaven."

The more significant impact of a theology that teaches an end-times doomsday scenario is that it has contributed to preachers' unwillingness to address the environment from the pulpit. It is to this day, seldom actually preached on Sunday morning in our churches. Why? A hostile relationship between faith and science has made climate change a victim of the origins debate. An illogical syllogism goes like this: Scientists believe in evolution and evangelicals reject evolution; therefore, evangelicals reject the scientific consensus on global warming.

This makes no sense, of course, but that many people think is does is all too true. Only 37% of evangelicals believe that climate change is human-induced – not that these evangelicals are likely to have had a serous conversation with an environmentalist. No need for that, because we can listen to AM talk radio or FOX-TV for the information we need. After all, why not listen to Rush Limbaugh for one's scientific knowledge? He has railed for years at those "environmental whackos" and identifies with us by waving the Christian flag as much as the American one.

Pardon me, but realism forces me to acknowledge that we as evangelicals have substituted personalities in the news/entertainment industry for credentialed scientists. The only way to bridge this gap is to bring scientists and evangelicals together. And that's exactly what we have done with our "Scientist-Evangelical" retreats and expeditions co-sponsored by the NAE and the Harvard Center on Health and the Global Environment.

This past year, Nobel laureate Eric Chivian and I co-hosted a meeting of 30 evangelical leaders and the nation's leading environmental scientists. One of the most powerful voices at that gathering (now called the "Thomasville Rebellion" and named for the town in rural Georgia where we met), was Gus Speth, Dean of the Yale School of Forestry and the Environment. Here's what he said at that event:

> Thirty years ago, I thought that with enough good science, we would be able to solve the environmental crisis. I was wrong. I used to think the greatest problems threatening the planet were pollution, bio-diversity loss and climate change. I was wrong there too. I now believe that the greatest problems are pride, apathy and greed. Because that's what's keeping us from solving the environmental problem. For that, I now see that we need a cultural and spiritual transformation. And we in the scientific community don't know how to do that. But you evangelicals do. We need your help.

Well, we as evangelical leaders are committed to offering that help. You can discover how these two communities have come to agreement about protecting creation by reading our statement, "An Urgent Call to Action: Scientists and Evangelicals Unite to Protect Creation," released January 17, 2007, at the National Press Club in Washington, DC. Furthermore, many scientists, led by E.O. Wilson, the leading environmental scientist of our time, have agreed to refer to the earth as "the creation" once again. And yet another example of bridge-building between the faith-and-science divide is PBS's October 2007 episode of its excellent *NOW* series, "God and Global Warming."

The era of accusations and name-calling has come to an end. The era of cooperation is at hand, and none too soon. But an even more significant accomplishment will occur when the worlds of religion and science come together in a new spirit of reconciliation. We still disagree, many of us, about how the world came into existence. But there's no disagreement about whether that world deserves protection.

We are on the verge of an evangelical awakening to the global environmental crisis. This crisis is evident by the pollution that lands heavy on the poor, the unprecedented loss of biodiversity, the warming of the average temperature of the planet leading to rising sea levels, increased flooding in low-lying coastal regions, an increase in insect-borne diseases, and severe droughts in many regions. Together, we intend to collaborate to urge our nation's political leaders to act on this crisis. We will roll up our sleeves to become part of the solution. There is no other option but to succeed.

**NOTE:** *In December 2008, Rev. Cizik resigned his position with NAE.*

## 2

THE REV. FRED SMALL

SENIOR MINISTER, FIRST CHURCH UNITARIAN

LITTLETON, MA

# The Greater Sacrifice

"We who are anguished by the earth's
injuries are no longer scorned eccentrics.
We are the emerging majority."

The burly African American officer was surprisingly gentle as he bound my hands behind my back with plastic handcuffs. Escorting me to the police van, he said quietly, "Please pray for me. I feel terrible arresting a minister. My family will never forgive me!"

It was May 3, 2001, one of those "blue true dream of sky" days that remind us of the astonishing beauty of creation. And I was going to jail.

Religious Witness for the Earth had been organizing barely three months. With the new administration in Washington dismissing scientific evidence of global warming and pressing to open the

Arctic National Wildlife Refuge to oil development, we could not remain silent. It was time to take our prayers out of the sanctuary and into the streets.

Over fifty of us from as far away as California and Alaska converged on Washington to tell Congress and the administration that climate change is a sin and despoiling the Arctic Refuge a sacrilege. After two days of issue briefings and lobbying on Capitol Hill, we gathered at the Department of Energy for a service of prayer and witness. Four police vans, a half-dozen cruisers and dozens of uniformed officers were waiting. Joined by local supporters, our congregation swelled to nearly 150: clergy in robes and stoles and clerical collars, rabbis in embroidered yarmulkes, parents and children and students, many carrying hand-lettered signs that read "Environmental Justice," "The Earth Is the Lord's," and "Thou Shalt Not Steal the Future."

Rev. Dr. Andrea Ayvazian, a United Church of Christ minister and Dean of Religious Life at Mount Holyoke College, opened the service with a spirit-filled song: "Lord, prepare me to be a sanctuary, pure and holy, tried and true, and with thanksgiving I'll be a living sanctuary for you." Our harmonies echoed over the plaza, bouncing off the cement walls and soaring overhead.

Rev. Bob Massie, an Episcopal priest and Executive Director of the Coalition for Environmentally Responsible Economies (CERES), read from Isaiah: "The earth dries up and withers, the world languishes and withers; the heavens languish together with the earth. The earth lies polluted under its inhabitants; for they have transgressed laws, violated the statutes, broken the everlasting covenant." (24:4,5)

The late Jonathon Solomon, a Gwich'in (the northernmost Indian Nation) elder, spoke of the land so sacred to his people that they are forbidden to visit there, lest they leave a footprint. Rev. Adora Iris Lee, Minister for Environmental Justice for the United Church of Christ, led us in passionate prayer. Rabbi Art Waskow read in Hebrew and English from Psalm 24. Rabbi Fred Scherlinder Dobb argued the religious imperative to care for creation.

As the service ended and the singing continued, 22 of us walked hand in hand to the entrance of the Department of Energy. There we knelt in prayer or stood in witness. Some of us prayed aloud for forgiveness for our mistreatment of creation and for wisdom and courage to protect it. As an officer of the Federal Protective Service gave us a first, second and third warning that we were subject to arrest, we continued to pray and sing. Finally the order was given, and the officers moved in swiftly to arrest us.

Uplifted by the power of the prayers and songs, I felt at once proud and humble, excited and serene, nervous and calm, solemn and joyful. Convinced of the justice of our actions, I felt our arrests were a kind of sacrament. I doubt I have ever felt more in communion with the divine and with all beings. Looking out from the van, I saw an 80-year-old elder of my church led away in handcuffs, and tears filled my eyes.

It's impossible to know the impact of our civil disobedience that day, or of the many acts of public witness we have performed since. The Arctic Refuge is still protected, but global warming accelerates.

While we seek always to be effective, we recall Thomas Merton's counsel "to concentrate not on the results but on the value, the rightness, the truth of the work itself. . . . The real hope, then, is not in something we think we can do but in God who is making something good out of it in some way we cannot see." (from a 1966 letter to James Forest, the Catholic peace activist). Merton, a Trappist monk, echoed the Bhagavad Gita, the ancient Hindu scripture: "Action alone is within your control, it never extends to the fruits. Be not attached to the fruits of action, nor be attached to inaction." (2:47) Global warming calls us to act.

"We are caught in an inescapable network of mutuality," wrote Rev. Dr. Martin Luther King, Jr., "tied in a single garment of destiny." Dr. King understood the essence of ecology: We belong to each other. Today, people of faith around the world are coming to understand that threats to the environment are threats to the principles of justice and compassion at the core of every religion.

Automobile fuel economy is an environmental issue. But when our dependence on cheap gasoline drives a tanker aground, and the spreading slick deprives an Inuit family of seal meat, that's an issue of justice and compassion.

Recycling is an environmental issue. But when a Chicago woman who's never smoked cigarettes gets lung cancer from breathing fumes from an incinerator burning recyclable trash, that's an issue of justice and compassion.

Deforestation is an environmental issue. But when tree root systems no longer hold soil in place and a mudslide sweeps away a peasant village, that's an issue of justice and compassion.

Energy conservation is an environmental issue. But when our tax dollars subsidize prison construction instead of green job training that could keep at-risk teens out of prison, that's an issue of justice and compassion.

Climate change is an environmental issue. But when people on the island nation of Tuvalu must abandon their homeland before it is swallowed by the sea, that's an issue of justice and compassion.

As we awake to the dangers of global warming, we realize that our profligate use of fossil fuels offends our most fundamental religious precepts.

Every religious tradition teaches awe of creation, yet we desecrate it. Every religious tradition teaches temperance in sensation and material things, yet we pursue them addictively, vainly hoping to fill our spiritual emptiness. Every religious tradition forbids theft, yet every day we live unsustainably we steal from our children and our children's children.

Throughout the world, poor and working people, and especially people of color, are pollution's first victims. They are the least equipped to mitigate the impacts of global warming, and will be the first to join the masses of environmental refugees.

"You have built houses of hewn stone," said the prophet Amos, "but you shall not live in them; you have planted pleasant vineyards, but you shall not drink their wine." (5:11) In years to come, as our children contend with the deadly consequences of global warming, they will ask us the same terrible questions asked after the abolition of slavery, after the fall of Third Reich, after the civil rights movement finally put an end to the shame of legal segregation — the same awful and incredulous questions asked of every human being complacent in the face of evil:

How could you not have known?

Knowing what you knew, how could you wait so long?

It's so easy to dwell on what's wrong. "One of the penalties of an ecological education," wrote Aldo Leopold in 1953, "is that one lives alone in a world of wounds." (from the 1953 essay, "The Round River: A Parable") We who are anguished by the earth's injuries are no longer scorned eccentrics. We are the emerging majority.

But we have far to go and little time to get there. Vast concentrations of power are arrayed to defend the status quo upon which they teeter. As Frederick Douglass told us, "Power concedes nothing without a demand. It never did and it never will." (from an August 3, 1857 speech in Canandaigua, New York) Individual acts of environmental responsibility — consuming less, recycling more, driving a fuel-efficient car — are necessary, but not sufficient to meet the challenge before us. Even if a vast simplicity movement succeeded in reducing demand for nonrenewable resources, without other intervention, reduced demand would drive down the price of these resources, stimulating the appetite of consumers still trapped in thrall of thingdom.

Personal responsibility is essential — but it is not sufficient. In and of itself, it fails to challenge the entrenched interests of corporations and the governmental agencies that collude with them. Just as the individual acts of conscience by slaveholders who freed their own slaves would never alone have brought an end to slavery, our individual lifestyle choices will not alone solve our environmental problems. And just as in the 1960s it was absurd to imagine that all we needed to do to end American apartheid was to have a personal transformative conversation with every racist in the United States, so we cannot rely on voluntary corporate change alone to solve the environmental crisis.

We need strong international treaties and tough state and federal laws that put all of us on the same playing field with the same rules. We need to pay a price for goods and services that reflects their actual cost to the environment, not merely that of production. This cannot be done without bold and comprehensive action by our government.

Changing a light bulb is good. Changing a member of Congress is better. Turning the tide against global warming will require the largest, most diverse, most creative and most courageous mass movement in human history.

For all our dedication, for all our effort, for all our love, we may not prevail. The human race may not survive the insults we have inflicted upon the earth. "As for prophecies, they will come to an end; as for tongues, they will cease; as for knowledge, it will come to an end." But "love never ends." (I Corinthians 3:8)

Two hundred and fifty million years ago, at the end of the Permian period, for reasons no one knows, ninety percent of the earth's species became extinct. Since then, there have been five more periods of massive extinction, including the present one. Each time, nature has somehow rebounded in astonishing abundance, diversity, and beauty. No doubt it will again. Whether the human species will be part of the picture is uncertain.

Perhaps the mantle of intelligence, creativity and productivity will be passed to another species that will be kinder, wiser, more farsighted than our own. In the long run, the earth will be just fine, and when its time, too, finally passes, surely other worlds will carry on the great adventure of consciousness. But we cannot stand by as the human race destroys itself, its habitat, and countless other species.

On April 4, 1967, one year to the day before his assassination, Martin Luther King Jr. addressed a meeting of Clergy and Laity Concerned at Riverside Church in New York City. Denouncing the war in Vietnam, his words speak as well to the challenge of global warming:

> We are now faced with the fact, my friends, that tomorrow is today. We are confronted with the fierce urgency of now. In this unfolding conundrum of life and history, there is such a thing as being too late. Procrastination is still the thief of time. Life often leaves us standing bare, naked, and dejected with a lost opportunity. . . . Over the bleached bones and jumbled residues of numerous civilizations are written the pathetic words, "Too late." . . . Now let us begin. Now let us rededicate ourselves to the long and bitter, but beautiful, struggle for a new world.

To stem our slide toward extinction, the easy and comfortable measures are no longer adequate. It's time to do the harder thing, the longer reach, the greater sacrifice to defend the earth and the sweet imperiled experiment called humanity.

3

THE REV. PAT WATKINS
UNITED METHODIST PASTOR
RICHMOND, VIRGINIA

# Building Creation on a Firm Foundation

"I never try to appeal to people of faith by talking about global warming or the Chesapeake Bay or mountaintop-removal coal mining, as important as those issues are. I start with the faith in order to build a solid foundation for this ministry. Then and only then is it effective to begin a conversation about the issues."

In spite of the fact that I grew up outside, in the woods or splashing in a creek, spending as much time in God's creation as my mother would allow, I would not have considered myself an environmentalist. I suppose, looking back, I took it for granted. We all lived that way in my hometown back then. There was nothing odd or unusual about spending most of our time outside; only now, by contrast to our current culture, does it seem strange that children would spend as much time outside as I did. I grew up connected to the earth, but I guess I thought that was just the way it was supposed to be.

It was later in life, as a missionary in Nigeria, that my environmentalism began to take real shape. Very soon upon arrival in our village of Bambur, my wife and I discovered that we had no choice but to live our lives in a way that was far more connected to the cycles of the earth than we ever had before. Bambur was small and remote: no electricity, no phone, no running water. Houses were tiny and round and made of mud bricks and thatched roofs. We had a mango tree in our backyard and could eat the fruit fresh from the tree when it was in season — but when it wasn't we couldn't just go to a grocery store and buy a mango from South America. Instead, we simply made do without.

A couple of times a year we went to the nearest big city to buy supplies, but we could only go during the dry season. There is a rainy season and a dry season in Nigeria. In the rainy season, the rivers fill with water, and since the dirt roads went straight through the rivers (there were no bridges), the water was too deep for our Land Cruiser to cross. In fact, we had to plan all our trips during the dry season, as it was impossible to get out any other time. We were forced to live our lives in relationship to the way the earth lives her life. The earth dictated to us rather than vice versa. For the first time in our memory, rather than living in such a way that we could at least isolate ourselves from the earth, if not actually manipulate its forces, we had to live in harmony with it. We discovered that not only was it possible to live connected to the cycles of earth, there was something really good about it. And then I began to think there was something even sacred about it.

I returned home from those years in Bambur with a burning question in my heart and mind: "Is there some connection between my faith and this new-found relationship to God's creation?" I began to take classes in Environmental Science and Ecology, while at the same time refreshing my theological background by reading the Bible again, looking for all the verses I could find that might provide an answer. After a couple of years of study, I decided the answer was a resounding "yes." There is an enormous amount of evidence, both Biblical and within church tradition, that supports my discovery that life in harmony with God's creation is fundamental to Christianity. In fact, up until a few hundred years ago, Christianity has never existed within any other paradigm. A close relationship to God's creation is nothing new for the church; we've simply forgotten it as we, in the United States at least, have become more and more isolated from creation.

It is purely and simply my faith as a Christian that compels me to care for God's creation. It is not optional; it's a requirement. God's creation is not merely an issue to which the church needs to pay some attention from time to time. It is much more fundamental to who we are as Christians. Throughout Christian history, a relationship with God requires us to be in relationship with each other. I believe that it is equally as necessary for Christians that a relationship with God requires a relationship with God's creation.

## LOOKING THROUGH THE LENS OF CREATION

Biblical evidence for these relationships is overwhelming. Space does not allow an exegetical analysis of the Hebrew and Christian scriptures, but several themes are apparent:

*God created the universe.* There are myriad different interpretations as to how exactly God did it, but Christians, as well as adherents of most other religions around the world, have a notion of a creator God.

*God continues to have a relationship with creation.* God used the non-human natural world numerous times to accomplish God's mission.

*God loves creation.* God made a covenant, not only with humanity but also with the earth itself. If God cares enough for the earth to make such a covenant and if we are to be people of God, how can we not make such a covenant ourselves? How can we not also express our love for the earth as God has done?

*God owns creation.* Biblically, creation was never a gift given to us to do with as we please. Creation belongs to God — always has and always will. If we could come to grips with that theological premise, it would change for the better the way we choose to live in relationship to creation.

*Creation praises God.* Obviously for the Biblical writers, God has a relationship with creation such that creation itself has the ability to praise God. Consider the words of Psalm 96: "Let the heavens be glad, and let the earth rejoice; let the sea roar, and all that fills it; let the field exult, and everything in it. Then shall all the trees of the forest sing for joy before the Lord." The praise of God is not a uniquely human endeavor. If creation itself has some kind of relationship with God, if creation knows God, how can we not respect that relationship?

*Creation reveals God.* Christians are not nature worshippers; however, the scriptures are clear that one way for humanity to recognize God is to examine the things God has made.

*Our relationships with creation and each other are connected.* Our responsibility to care for the poor and disenfranchised affects how we relate to creation. In other words, we must relate to creation in such a way as to provide for the poor instead of continuing to harm the poor disproportionately due to the improper ways we have chosen to relate to creation.

*Creation reflects human obedience and disobedience to God.* Biblical writers perceived natural phenomena as God's response to humanity either obeying or disobeying God. Similarly, today the natural world responds to humanity's care or abuse of creation, indirectly commenting on our responsibility to be good stewards of that which belongs to God.

*Jesus is part of creation.* The New Testament contains writings that suggest Jesus was a part of creation from the very beginning. He demonstrated power over creation and felt especially close to God in the natural world. Paul's writings suggest Jesus was the redeemer of all of creation, not just humanity.

Finally, the Bible contains numerous suggestions as to how humanity can actually live in a good relationship with creation. God stated rules that govern how humanity and creation are to live together in harmony. Both the Old and New Testaments include visions of a new creation, a creation that reflects a right relationship between humanity and creation, and between humanity and God. Jesus provided stories of stewardship examples of how we can get along with each other and with the earth. Here are just two, from Matthew and Luke:

> *Do not store up for yourselves treasures on earth, where moth and rust consume and where thieves break in and steal; but store up for yourselves treasures in heaven, where neither moth nor rust consumes*

*and where thieves do not break in and steal. For where your treasure is, there your heart will be also. (Matthew 6:19-21)*

And,

*And he [Jesus] said to them, "Take care! Be on your guard against all kinds of greed; for one's life does not consist in the abundance of possessions." Then he told them a parable: "The land of a rich man produced abundantly. And he thought to himself, 'What should I do, for I have no place to store my crops?' Then he said, 'I will do this: I will pull down my barns and build larger ones, and there I will store all my grain and my goods. And I will say to my soul, 'Soul, you have ample goods laid up for many years; relax, eat, drink, be merry.' But God said to him, 'You fool! This very night your life is being demanded of you. And the things you have prepared, whose will they be?' So it is with those who store up treasures for themselves but are not rich toward God." (Luke 12:15-21)*

The problem is not that we have no Biblical or historical traditions of creation care; the problem is that our isolation from God's creation makes us read the Bible with blinders on. As we study the scriptures, we simply miss the richness that is right in front of us because God's creation is no longer on our radar screens. To put it another way, we're not looking through the lens of creation. It's not that we've become bad people; we're just not aware of all the Bible has to say on this subject, because we're not looking for it. And we don't look for it because we've lost our connection to the natural world.

## WORSHIP AND GOD'S CREATION

As a prerequisite to anything the church chooses to do in its ministry to God's creation, it must first recover a Biblically and theologically based relationship to creation. Sure we can quit using Styrofoam, start recycling and change our light bulbs. But if that is where we start, we've missed the spiritual meaning of a relationship with God's creation that enhances our relationship with God. While this ministry to God's creation is about saving the planet, it is first and foremost about faith. I never try to appeal to people of faith by talking about global warming or the Chesapeake Bay or mountaintop-removal coal mining, as important as those issues are. I start with the faith in order to build a solid foundation for this ministry. Then and only then is it effective to begin a conversation about the issues.

After establishing the Biblical foundation for creation care, the obvious question emerges: "So what?" We have this faith thing going on, this God thing. We've established the fact that Christianity requires a relationship with God's creation if we are really to be in relationship with God, but what does that mean for the church? How do we as Christians live out our faith in relationship to God's creation? Do we have to start worshipping the trees? (I don't think that's necessary.) Do we have to get naked and start dancing around the churchyard under the full moon? (It might be fun but I don't think that's what God is calling us to do either.) So what is next? Where do we go with this fresh understanding of our faith?

The task is to incorporate a relationship to God's creation into everything we do as people of faith. We're so tempted to go for those funny looking light bulbs, and that's good, but there's more to it than that. God's creation has to be honored in worship. The sacredness of creation has to enter the sanctuary. Through worship, we enable creation itself to praise God along with all of us. Worship grounds us in the faith; thus it has to ground us in God's creation as well. Worship can connect us to God, each other, and creation. It can enable us to realize that we're all in this together, that God's love for each of us is the same as God's love for every-thing else God created, and that our love for God has to include love for creation as well. Worship is the center of our being, of our life in Christ. There can be no more effective way to re-introduce us to a relationship to God's creation than through worship.

And we must educate. Education complements worship. It gives legs to our faith as expressed in worship. Through education in the church, we learn how to apply the faith to the environmental issues out there. Global warming can be seen through the lens of science and politics, which is fine. But it can also be seen through the lens of faith. Faith will move us like nothing else can. To work for policy and lifestyle change because of the science of the green-house effect will lead to some changes, but to work for those same things because as Christians we have to do all in our power to care for and heal God's creation, is a whole different thing. Our actions may be the same, but our motivation has to be different, from a faith perspective. For me, bringing global warming into the world of faith is to bring it into the place where I am most at home. It is from a context of faith that I truly feel as if I can do something about global warming.

## BRINGING IT ALL TOGETHER

Here's how it works: The solution to the problem of global warm-ing is to emit less carbon. (Please indulge the Global Warming 101 for just a moment.) Fewer carbon emissions will require the con-sumption of less fossil fuel. Less fossil fuel consumption means less driving, a switch to more fuel-efficient vehicles, and less use of fossil-fuel-based electricity. Meanwhile, we're doing more planting and cutting down fewer trees. The concept is simple.

The reasons that would motivate any of us to make these changes are numerous: Alleviating the negative effects of global warming is an obvious one. But of course there are others...better air and water quality that would enhance human health, making the US energy independent and able to negotiate global relationships from a better position, preserving the beauty of the earth or just saving money (especially as the price of oil goes up and up), preserving animal habitat (if we preserved our forests we would enhance the habitat of God's creatures and prevent yet more extinctions at our hand), saving precious fossil fuel and other non-renewable resources in consideration of the generations to come, and the list goes on and on and on.

All of these reasons are good and worthwhile, but the best reason by far, in my opinion as a person of faith, is simply because I am a Christian and my faith in a creator God compels me to do all in my power to care for creation. So I will use less fossil fuel, tread lightly and protect our precious resources, but the reason why I do it is because of my faith in Christ. Christians understand this power of faith. And by bringing education into the church, we can equip ourselves Biblically and theologically to make the connection between our faith and the issues out there.

As we think about education in the church, let's not overlook the importance of bringing this message to children who, because they seldom go outside anymore, are losing their connection with the earth. Our church camps, for example, can be a fantastic way to teach children about ecology in a rich and meaningful way, and to simply connect them to God's creation. Perhaps they will connect with God in the process. What an incredible gift the church can give to our children and, consequently, to creation as well.

The church can send a compelling message as a witness to environmental lifestyle changes: Those funny looking light bulbs will make a difference when churches take the lead in making the switch; so too will instituting a recycling program, energy-use targets, solar and wind energy installations. If we could total up the carbon footprint of our churches and our church activities, we would probably be shocked at how high that number really is. The church can amplify its positive contributions to the faith community by using its own commitment to the earth as a platform from which to educate its families about how they too can lessen their impact on God's creation.

Historically, churches have always been about mission. This comes out of our relationship with God, and thus our relationship to each other. We have been in mission to people all over the world for centuries. As we recover a good relationship with God's creation, we will begin to see environmental issues included in the mission of the church, the same way caring for the poor has traditionally been.

This mission can be carried out in two ways: direct service and political advocacy. An example of service would be for a congregation to clean up a stream in its community or to plant a garden on the church grounds to feed the poor. Not only would they be fulfilling their traditional mission to care for the poor, but by making better use of the land itself, they would also be caring for God's creation. Likewise, political advocacy has traditionally been no stranger to people of faith. The task is to broaden our scope of advocacy to include environmental legislation in addition to legislation that provides a better life for all of God's people. And we're learning that, today, it is hard to have one without the other because of the connections between environmental degradation and the disproportionately negative effects on the poor, especially in the Third World. An example I can imagine at home is for churches in Virginia, where I live, to declare the Chesapeake Bay as a mission field and to commit to its healing, whether through service, advocacy, or both.

Faith is hope. Faith provides hope for both creation and humanity. As creation becomes re-incorporated into everything the church says and does, creation will once again be able to praise God because of the amazing work we will have done to re-establish a good, positive relationship with it. We see ourselves, liberal, moderate, evangelical, conservative, all coming together with concerns about creation. We're bringing great diversity to creation's table. Not only are we beginning to incorporate different theologies and faiths into our conversation, science is doing the same thing by helping us understand the inter-connectedness of the natural world. We're all in this together. We depend on each other and on creation itself. Biblically there are visions of what creation can become. We have the responsibility to fulfill the vision and I have no doubt that we, as people of faith, will accomplish the task.

## 4

RABBI ANDREA COHEN-KIENER
SPIRITUAL LEADER OF CONGREGATION PNAI OR (JEWISH RENEWAL)
HARTFORD, CONNECTICUT

# Reaching into History and Finding the Future

"We are the first generation to possess the knowledge
that we can erase ourselves from terrestrial life."

෧෨

My life-long defining "isms" came upon me in my second year of college: Judaism, feminism and environmentalism. They came at the same time but they did not come together. No, they came in three different packages, each mostly suspicious of the other.

Judaism bid me to look into the long story of my people's dialog with God and with human history. From the stories, from the rituals and from the connection, I could cull a kind of reality map that gave meaning, depth and texture to my life. Though I grew up in a Jewish-identified home, we had more of a cultural identity than a religious one. The awakening of Jewish identity in college gave a spiritual substance and a religious practice to the bones of my Judaism.

And I am female. What that meant was being redefined by the minute, as women thinkers and their allies explored inequities in social power structures right down to the minutiae of the words we used to name God. Judaism and feminism challenged each other; each raised important questions about my essential being. After decades of struggling, I came to appreciate the particularities of *Jewish* feminism — a feminism that asked me to create new rituals and teachings that were authentic to me, rather than solely imitating the masculine role models, which form the bulk of the written tradition.

From feminism I learned to know deeply that what is is not necessarily what is right or best. And from feminism I learned to sit with the stretch of a difficult question.

And environmentalism. We are the first generation to possess the knowledge that we can erase ourselves from terrestrial life. That is a power we are much too disorganized and immature to have. Yet, there it is. From environmentalism and the interface with feminism I learned that to honor our bodies compels us to honor our collective body, the earth.

These "new sciences" of feminism and environmentalism directed new questions to the Jewish tradition, which has, after all, a venerated history of questioning. One found that it was necessary to angle the Talmud or Bible text just a bit to the right or to the side, to glimpse the contours of a cohesive answer.

An example: Torah does not have a *mitzvah*, or a commandment, about recycling. We have 613 commandments. We have commandments about beard styles and the milking of cows. But recycling? No. And of course this is so: Recycling mandates were not a question in Torah and Talmudic consciousness as they developed in the Middle East over the centuries. Waste was an anathema; it was stupid. When a human community lives so close to the limits of survival, waste is barely possible to imagine. When one seeks guidance about environmental issues from the Jewish tradition, it becomes necessary to look for implicit values and intention. It is necessary to filter current events through an older prism.

There *are* commandments about quality of life, however. There are laws about the limits of destruction, even in war. There is a vast body of laws that weigh individual freedoms against communal norms and safety (a central issue in much environmental activism today!). There is a prohibition against harming oneself. There is a commandment to preserve life.

There is a vibrant knowing of God in the treatises of Judaism. Rambam, Moses Maimonides, our great sage of the Middle Ages, would say that if we must love the Creator, we must know the Handiwork: All That Is. Science, religion and awe were one for him.

There is a pattern in the Jewish calendar of celebration that places us in the cycle of seasons. This witnesses an ancient humanness that is easily lost with the advent of indoor lighting and an abundant year-round food supply. The blessing of food is an enduring pattern in Judaism. And there is the Sabbath.

Each of these practices and sensibilities witness a deeply environmental Jewish ethic. But for real guidance, we need to sit with the new questions and the old traditions and see what we can make of it all. As an environmentalist, a feminist and a Jew, I find my self reaching into history to find future. I find myself whispering, or sometimes raging, new questions, and then sitting — waiting for The Word to bounce off the mountains and reach back to my ears.

In this way, I feel, my tradition becomes more alive. It continues. It is relevant.

My first step into Judaism was thus. Rabbi Arthur Waskow, now a dear colleague, then a firebrand activist that I had heard of, was conducting a campaign against the use of napalm in Vietnam and Cambodia because of Deuteronomy 20:19: "When you lay siege to a city and wage war against it a long time to capture it, you must not destroy its trees, wielding an ax against any food producing tree." (from *The Living Torah*, Rabbi Aryeh Kaplan). When I heard about Arthur's campaign, it hit me for the first time that we really are supposed to seek a way to live these laws.

So I find myself in the land of a vibrant Jewish, feminist environmental consciousness and I am not alone. The teaching of feminism has percolated into a generation of thinkers. And more of us hear the cry of the earth: the shared despair and collective disconnection, the morbid fear of what we all may face if we do not find the brakes on the economic engines of pollution and climate change. The evermore visible consequences of the havoc we wreak call more of us to consciousness and action on behalf of the earth.

In this time, you don't have to be a pagan to speak about earth in your worship service. I am in the company of people of every faith who feel the call to love God by walking lightly, responsibly on earth.

So, from the early years of conflict between my isms, I am in a rich time. I have a wider context and mission for my Jewish practice. And I have a deep spiritual grounding for my environmental work.

I am the director of Connecticut's Interfaith Power and Light. It is my job to cull colleagues for this massive work. If I didn't have access to the pulpit, I could barely allow myself to feel the degradation of our life supporting systems. But from the pulpit I can call out to my community and beyond. We will need so many to steer us off our current course towards destruction. Each faith community has its own language for the call to earth care. I've heard nuns speak of composting as additional proof of life after death. I've heard Episcopalians speak of expressing God's love to the least among us, down to the bugs and microbes.

When I first began approaching my Jewish colleagues in my role as director of an interfaith environmental group, around 2002, I found many individuals who were equally passionate about care of creation. Most of them felt frustrated within the context of their congregations. When I called synagogues, I was often told "Oh, you need to talk to Louise!" or "That's what Meryl is interested in…" and I was referred to the one person in a 500-family congregation who was known to resonate with this issue.

I began to think of my religion as an "ethnic church;" of course Judaism is neither an ethnicity nor a church. But the Jewish body – in those early days – responded to this issue no differently than the Korean Baptists and the Spanish Catholics and the black Evangelicals. Here are populations who have another skin of identity around their religious affiliations. They have had legitimate and pressing needs specific to their own communities.

For many, the environment has been viewed as a "leisure issue" for more comfortable communities, those without pressing survival concerns, such as poverty, housing, discrimination, etc.

Over time, as the environmental implications of our collective economies have become more obvious, ostriches everywhere are pulling their heads out of the sand to see what's coming over the horizon. The central agency for Jewish polity, Jewish Council for Public Affairs, added energy independence and climate-change action to their list of policy items in 2007. Care of creation became an internal Jewish issue and I began to see more individuals, more rabbis and more Tikkun Olam/Social Justice Committees, take on environmental issues and actions. The consciousness of Jewish environmentalism has been around for decades, but now we are seeing a deeper internalization of related advocacy, celebration and practice.

There is still a particular hesitancy among some in the Jewish community to participate in an interfaith project. There are natural barriers and suspicions in new coalitions. And there are language and framework challenges. For most North Americans, the religious language is Christian. Even in an interfaith setting, perhaps even especially in an interfaith setting, celebrants and preachers may barely notice if they have slipped into religious language that is not wide enough to include non-Christians. This is a theological challenge for all of us in the work of religious environmentalism. We have to find a way to speak to our own faith family in a language that is strong, passionate and familiar. Yet we also have to speak to each other in a way that is wider, and more inclusive. For many of us, our God will get bigger as our God language expands. In addition to our finely tuned denominational version of theology, when we expand our view of history to include cosmic and geologic history, our God idea is bigger. The imperative to collective action helps us feel new possibilities. We'll be more effective together.

There is one more issue that is a challenge to us all and that is the big bugaboo of consumerism or capitalism: I realized long ago that inviting people to move back into caves to save the planet is not going to be popular. Nor was I going to be effective if I went around shaming people about the material wealth that they had. You can't clean up the natural environment by mucking up the emotional field. But I'm religious! I believe that God is Oneness. So if we really are mucking up the physical environment, we are probably feeling that pain on other levels as well. I decided to try to "name the pain."

Many of us suffer from loneliness and despair, from a lack of connection and purpose. I believe a good bit of the drive in us – which beckons us to consume, go, do, buy – is a kind of escaping from inner agitation. We know we cannot quell a spiritual hunger with a new Audi; that kind of hunger is filled by purpose and by meaningful connection. Wealth is not bad, but wealth accumulated to stave off emptiness and fear is no blessing. It is an awesome tool if we tithe, if we invest in best practices and best technologies. Wealth is a powerful ally and a blessing, when we invest it in enduring ways.

So I call myself out first on my relationship with materialism. This is a legitimate religious pursuit. Are we not all engaged in some struggle between body and spirit? How much is enough? What brings me enduring pleasure? How rich is my "village" of relationships? Then I want to challenge rapacious capitalism and measure my bounty with a new bottom line of value and sustainability. At the end of the day, I believe we will all choose the health of our children's future over one new, shiny thing.

The many impacts of the material economy, such as it is, accumulate. None of us is immune from the cancers and asthmas, nor from the change of tides and seasons. We are ripping down mountainsides and dwarfing them with our garbage heaps. How long can this go on?

I believe that when we see, feel and name all of these disconnections – from self, from earth, from other – and recognize how integral they are, we will see the better choice more clearly. We will begin to reclaim a kind of natural and social health and wealth. A little more and a little more. More cooperation. More sharing. More gardening. More honoring ancient ways. More regional food ways. More locally grown music. More simple foods. More community.

These little pieces of the solution are seeds. They can offer us a hundred-fold return if they are well planted and supported. Life here is resilient; it will grow and continue in some form. But still it is vital that as we grow along with it, our vision is deep, deliberate and joyful. We have already hit some walls. There is damage to the vehicle. Let us learn to steer as skillfully as possible to avoid an even worse impact.

What an interesting, terrifying conundrum we have created for ourselves. We will have to go forward with faith and purpose. We will have to keep the thought of the common good before us. We will need prayer, and each other. There is a thrill in it.

In my religious language, this collectivity is messianic. Adam was a gardener. We reach into that past to find our future. May God bless the expanse of our consciousness. May Oneness inspire us and guide us. May Spirit help us find blessing in our work together. And may our actions serve the One.

5

THE REV. JIM DEMING
UNITED CHURCH OF CHRIST
NASHVILLE, TN

# From Southern Fried Guilt
# to Spiritual Responsibility

"Is there something I can learn from my 'born again' tradition,
born in the piney woods of East Texas and the rolling hills of
middle Tennessee? What keeps us on the path of environmental
righteousness and off the backslider's bench?"

૱

I first began working on climate change and global warming
with congregations in Arkansas and Tennessee in the fall of
2007. One evening, I showed Jeff Barrie's documentary *Kilowatt
Ours* and then led a general discussion afterwards. Soon after, it
became apparent that the reactions I was getting were more than
just "thank you" for new information. There seemed to be a stir-
ring within some of the participants that was deeper than a decision to change light bulbs and caulk windows. I sensed that some

41

began to acknowledge for the first time the real extent of damage we were causing to ourselves and God's creatures, and the threat to life on this planet for us, for our children and their children. And I sensed that they had begun to acknowledge their complicity and the great need for change. And then, I began to sense the proper focus of my pastoral care work.

Each of us has a history of how we came to a moment of insight. In the Southern religious tradition, we often talk about a "conversion experience" where we are "born again" and become a new person. Sermons are full of folk who have seen the light, changed their evil ways, and reformed their behavior to follow the paths of righteousness. Many of us in the South grew up with the tradition of altar calls, where confessions were public and emotional. But it seemed the "back-sliders" were just as numerous, trundling down the aisle once again as they confessed that they had, as the Apostle Paul says, done that which they ought not to have done and not done that which they should have.

What then, are we asking folks to do when we ask them to change more than their light bulbs? Is there something I can learn from my "born again" tradition, born in the piney woods of East Texas and the rolling hills of middle Tennessee? What keeps us on the path of environmental righteousness and off the backslider's bench?

I believe that we must understand that we are asking people to change their basic values, not just their light bulbs, and how we go about asking will have a profound effect on the success and longevity of this change. I believe that values are changed when our experiences and observations don't meet our presuppositions, and someone we trust invites us to a new vision of what could be. In this important moment in history, what we are asking of people is deep, for the climate crisis we are in is not just an inconvenient truth anymore; it is a transformational truth based on a new set of values, a new way of looking at the world.

Over the years, my values have undergone a transformation that would make any evangelist proud. I was born and grew up in Texas, where my father worked in the oil business for a division of Halliburton. I grew up in Texas culture where bigger is better, more is best, and food was always a smorgasbord of all you could eat and never just a single portion. It was the land of swagger and cars as big as a house and pick-up trucks that were a sign of virile manhood.

But somewhere in my growing up and transformation, I began to reject a value system based on excess, hyper-consumption and "me first." Maybe it began with my 9th-grade Sunday school teacher, Mrs. Oliver, who encouraged me to ask every question about everything, and made doubt OK. Maybe it was when I was in Seminary in Atlanta, and drove city busses as a summer job, I picked up people living in squalor in places with ironic names like Joyland and Highpoint Apartments. Maybe it was when our president lied to us again and again about the war in Vietnam that scarred so many of my generation. Whatever it was, my values changed because my experiences and my observations didn't match my presuppositions and because someone I trusted invited me to a new vision of what could be.

My Texas inspirations, the people I trusted, were people like Molly Ivins, one of the great political commentators who wrote with truth on one shoulder and humor on the other. She and Jim Hightower captured my imagination. He was the one who said of a

Texas legislator, "If ignorance goes to forty dollars a barrel, I want the drilling rights to his head." And then there was the great Texan and role model Barbara Jordan, whose address to the Democratic convention was absolutely spell-binding, and whose search for the unvarnished facts in the Watergate hearings about the duplicity of Richard Nixon was based on her love of the Constitution of the United States. For me, she was the definition of a true patriot.

So eventually my education brought me to a set of values that felt good deep down inside of me, and were even bigger than the state of Texas. They came from the prophet Micah, from whom I heard what God wants from me: to do justice, love kindness, and walk humbly with my God. When I saw the picture of our citizens sitting on their roofs after the flood of Katrina with the word "HELP" spelled out beside them, I knew that I needed to do something about a kind of injustice where those with means can leave and those without are left behind. When I see a culture bent on getting more quantities of stuff without any regard to how it will truly improve the quality of our lives, I know that kindness is a victim of a system that uses and abuses the natural environment. And when I am invited to walk humbly, then I begin to examine my own carbon footprint to see where I can be a role model for the values I espouse.

When I hear in the Gospels the two great commandments are to love God and love our neighbors as ourselves, I reflect that we have got the loving ourselves down pretty good. It's loving God and God's creation and our neighbor that we have trouble with. These are the values that should give me the foundation for all I do in life. And here is the catch for me and for you: *Your values are not your values unless you act on them.* They are verbal and not visceral unless you act on them. And what we are asking people to do is to transform their values at a visceral level and act on them.

I was reading about a young woman who decided to join the Sojourners community in Washington, DC and work in the inner city neighborhoods on issues of justice. Along the way, she caught the green bug and decided to be as green as she could be, recycling cans, riding public transportation, buying second-hand clothes and a host of other actions. She worked and worked at it but soon found it didn't bring her much peace after all, because, she said, she was still competitive about having things, and not having them was her way of competing with the dominant mindset of accumulation. What she began to realize is that real transformation is internal, where we begin to adopt a new set of values that determines what is really important and lasting in life, rather than what we are deprived of.

And that brings me to the question, what are we inviting people to be a part of? Is it better? And if it is, then we must invite people to see for themselves what it will be. In the wisdom literature of the Hebrew Scriptures, the sages say, "Without vision, the people perish." I absolutely agree, and so much of what we have been doing in the last 20 years since the first environmental movement is playing defense – reacting, rather than working toward a vision.

But now it is time to create that vision. Remember, values transformation really means moving from one set of values to another. We need to be positive and invite folks to join this growing movement by becoming those trusted people with a vision. The Sierra Club folks tell us that their research indicates that lots of people now know that global warming and climate change are real.

45

Of course there is still ignorance and there are talk-show wing nuts that make money off of scaring people. But lots of folks want to know what they can do, and many are waiting for an invitation from someone they trust to lead the way.

In his 2007 article in *Orion* magazine, "To Remake the World," Paul Hawken tells us that in his travels all over the world he meets thousands of people who are asking the right questions and working towards a new reality of sustainability. He says it is not yet an organized movement but rather an organic force born out of the need to survive on this planet. He says:

> *I have come to these conclusions: this is the largest social movement in all of history, no one knows its scope, and how it functions is more mysterious than meets the eye. What does meet the eye is compelling: tens of millions of ordinary and not-so-ordinary people willing to confront despair, power, and incalculable odds in order to restore some semblance of grace, justice, and beauty to this world.* (Orion, May/June 2007)

In his book *Deep Economy*, Bill McKibben says we are starting to see a movement in this country based on a European model set of values:

- From individual autonomy to community relationships,
- From assimilation to cultural diversity,
- From accumulation of wealth to quality of life,
- From unlimited material growth to sustainable development,
- From unrelenting toil to deep play, and
- From belongings to belonging.

This may be the set of values, the seeds of a vision, we are inviting people to move towards. If so, what we are inviting people to become a part of is positive, it is preferable, and it is possible.

But how do we get there? There are many differences between the first, and now the second, environmental movements, but I think the primary difference is that we need *everybody* to join this one. We can't leave it to the lawyers to sue the bad guys, we can't leave it to the Sierra Club and other advocacy groups to hound our politicians, we can't leave it to the Nature Conservancy and local land trusts to save our natural treasures. We need them for sure, but this is about transformation, not accommodation, of our entire culture, and I think we have to develop strategies that empower people, all people, at the grass-roots level.

Back in the eighties, I read a book that transformed my way of working. The book is called *The Long Haul*, by Myles Horton, who founded the Highlander Center in Tennessee. He worked to organize coal miners beginning in the 1930s, and then helped organize during the civil rights movement of the 1950s and '60s. A lot of folks think Rosa Parks just one day decided not to go to the back of the bus, but she was actually trained at the Highlander Center in non-violent civil disobedience. Myles Horton said that when you go into communities, you begin by listening and respecting. You are the resource person who can bring in new ideas and connections and resources, but ultimately, your job is to empower people to take control of their own situation, not to do it for them. People know that we can't eat the fish in the river because of mercury poisoning. They know they spend too much time in traffic away from their families. They know something is wrong. They just need some strategies and resources to take their own action to change what they can. I believe one of our most important and critical tasks ahead is to build new leadership at the grass-roots level, and then get out of the way.

When I worked in Ohio for the Rails-to-Trails Conservancy, I always tried to practice the teachings of Myles Horton, but sometimes I needed to be hit with a hammer to remember what my job was. I was invited to go down to southern Ohio — which is really Appalachian hill country — to talk to a group of citizens about building a railtrail. As they explained it to me over the phone, there was a 3-mile corridor between two rural towns that would be suitable both for an underground sewer line and an above-ground trail. When I walked into the smoke-filled room, I noticed immediately that I was the only one there not in overalls. Just about everybody had his or her arms crossed and wore a scowl.

And they put me through it. For about three hours, I answered question after question. I addressed their fears and affirmed their hopes and invited them to see other trail projects and talk to other communities. I said to them, "If you don't want it, it won't happen. But your kids and your grandkids will love you for providing a safe place to walk and ride bikes, and you'll see your neighbors getting the exercise they need to live longer and healthier lives." At the end of the meeting, just about everybody had come around. Then a gentleman who had to be about 100 came up to me and said, "Mr. Deming, someday me and my grandkids are gonna ride our horses on that trail." Well, I quickly countered what he said with something about how it's up to the community to decide if horses could be on the trail. And then he said very emphatically to me, "No sir. You didn't hear me. Someday me and my grandkids *are* gonna ride on that trail."

You see. I should have shut up. I planted the seed and held out the vision and he caught it. His values had changed, and now I needed to get the hell out of the way because it was his community to take care of, not mine.

My namesake and distant relative is W. Edwards Deming. He was a brilliant industrialist who went to Japan after World War II and helped rebuild their economy based on the value of quality. From reading about him and studying his methods, one thing he said struck a chord. He said that cars and trucks and airplanes took over from the railroads, and the railroads failed. He said the railroads always thought they were in the railroad business. But they were really in the transportation business.

Most of us environmentalists think we are in the environmental business, but we are really in the hope business. So many people now understand that their experiences and their observations no longer match their presuppositions, and they are looking for someone to hold out a new vision and inspire them to change. This is not just about changing light bulbs, though that is a good start. This is about changing values that ultimately change lives.

There will be times of backsliding and confession, but there will also be times of grace and insight that are God's reward for doing justice, loving kindness, and walking humbly *with* our God. Let us humbly *invite* our neighbor and walk *humbly* to the future together.

6

THE REV. DR. CLARE BUTTERFIELD
UNITARIAN UNIVERSALIST MINISTER
CHICAGO, ILLINOIS

# Faith in Place

"In our offices, tacked up to the wall, is our Illinois Department
of Agriculture meat broker's license. We think this is funny.
I don't remember meat broker day in seminary.
Maybe I was sick."

T here have been moments over the last nine years when I really
thought I was losing my sense of humor. I am a Unitarian
Universalist minister and the director of an interfaith environmental ministry where people believe pretty profoundly in a pretty long
list of things. But of all the important things on my own personal
list, the one I really don't think I can afford to lose is my sense of
humor.

At times it's been the only thing keeping the organization Faith
in Place alive. Like the day the wheelbarrow came through the

51

second-story window of the tiny, leaky offices we used to rent at a little church. It helped to find that funny.

Faith in Place exists to help congregations and communities of worship make earth stewardship part of their religious life. We create tools for religious people to become better stewards of creation. We've been around for almost ten years now, and we partner with hundreds of congregations of every possible faith. We also do double duty as the Illinois Interfaith Power and Light Campaign, so we find ourselves in the company of good people in many other states doing similar work. Lots of company these days. It wasn't always so.

## Getting Here

The idea that religious people have a stake in how we treat this gift of earth may seem obvious, but I can assure you that ten years ago it was a pretty hard sell in religious circles. It either wasn't on the radar screen, or it was actively resisted as a religious undertaking. Some suspected green religiosity of being paganism by another name.

John Chryssavgis, Eastern Orthodox scholar and writer, says in his book, *Light Through Darkness*:

*We are called to relearn the sense of communion or connectedness, that we are connected not only to one another, but also to the earth that binds us. And we will be judged, I believe, by the tenderness and delicacy with which we respond to nature — often a reflection of the way in which we treat human beings. Until and unless I am able to see in the face of the world the face of my own child, I will not be able to discern also in it the face of all faces, the face of my God. Then I can recognize in each tree and in each animal a face, and a name, and a time, and a place, and a voice that longs to be heard.*

So, what we are trying to do is not to change light bulbs. We are trying to change people — with the assumption that they will then be the kind of people who will change their own light bulbs. We will, in the end, save only what we love. We must learn again to love the places we inhabit, to know them like kin, which they are. We must see in the face of the earth the face of our own children. Then we will know what to do.

Interfaith environmental ministry is a way of exploring the religious undertaking in a particular context. It's an exercise in pragmatism. I am influenced, myself, by the school called process theology, and by the writers within that school who are also scientists. Process theology, to oversimplify, is a way of examining God and creation that emphasizes moments in time over objects in space, and an open-ended, unpredictable future that incorporates both order and novelty. I want to engage with the thinkers who have figured out how to be both biologists and believers, the ones that acknowledge the true scientific complexity and wonder of the natural world, and who see where God's activity might still have play. I am also a dyed-in-the-wool Midwesterner who loves this part of the country and who has spent most of her life here. This is my place that I love and will work to save. This is the place I know as if it were a part of my family. This is my personal context.

But I work with people who come from many different perspectives and places.

When I started I didn't know any of this. I didn't know where I was going or how to describe in theological language what I felt to be the unmediated presence of God when I stood in the presence of nature. Sure, I was already ordained as a minister in the faith that gave us the American Transcendentalist tradition (they believed in unmediated experiences of the divine in nature too). I started out with the conviction that the state of our planet was a moral issue, and that that it was relevant to everybody. It naturally followed that if I went out with high expectations for the people I met then good things were likely to happen.

People have been very kind and forgiving. Once I went to a meeting on the west side of Chicago — a low-income, high-crime, and predominantly African American neighborhood, where it's pretty obvious on sight that I'm a visitor — and I talked to some people at a community center there about farmers in a little town outside the city called Hopkins Park, in Pembroke Township. Pembroke Township is one of the poorest spots on the US map. Not all the houses there have indoor plumbing, heat or floors. Really. One of the women at the meeting said she'd support me because, as she said, "When I saw this little white lady coming in here talking about Pembroke," where she happened to be from, "I knew God was in this work." She told me, "Write down the vision — like in Habbakuk." I may be an ordained minister but I confess I didn't know that Habbakuk was even in the Bible. I looked it up. It's short (he was one of the lesser prophets): "Write the vision; make it plain on tablets, so that a runner may read it. For there is still a vision for the appointed time; it speaks of the end and does not lie. If it seems to tarry, wait for it; it will surely come, it will not delay." (Habbakuk 2:2)

I don't really think of myself as a messenger of God but I've been treated like one sometimes.

More often, I've been treated like an honored guest, in every kind of neighborhood and congregation. I've been served so very much tea by my Muslim hosts that I absolutely couldn't hold any more. I've been welcomed by hugs into churches quite different from my own. I must seem very harmless when I show up at the door. I wish people saw me as mighty, but I'll accept what they offer, in need of their protection.

When Faith in Place talks to a congregation the first thing we try to do is classify the problem correctly. We're trying to see all the pieces instead of just one part or another, and we're trying to get folks to see this work fundamentally as a religious activity — a practice of love. This is practicing what we preach, seeing all the implications and applications of the theologies we profess.

So the decision about whether to use compact fluorescent bulbs or incandescents in the church fixtures, or to serve the cheap coffee from Sam's Club or shade-grown organic fair trade coffee, is a religious decision that a religious body has to make. And the act of making those decisions in favor of least destruction is an act of restoring the body of the congregation to full communion with the world in which it resides.

So what decisions are we talking about with Faith in Place? They fall into two general categories: energy and food. On the energy side, we have our Illinois Interfaith Power and Light campaign (IPL). IPL's focus is global warming, and we work to mitigate that by helping congregations conserve energy and use renewable energy in place of the dirtier forms of energy that come from conventional sources. Around us, that means limiting the use of coal and nuclear for electricity, and natural gas for heat. We'd like to see congregations use solar thermal systems for hot water and geothermal systems for heat. We also want to make sure they aren't losing all their heat out through leaky windows and under-insulated roofs, and that they're switching to Energy Star® electric products. And then we'd like to see them purchase wind certificates or other forms of $CO_2$ offsets to make up for the conventional electricity they still use.

On the food side, we work directly with some local farmers to get their sustainably grown products into the hands of local consumers in a way that is humane to animals, good to the earth, fair to farmers and transparent to consumers. For example, we encourage Community Supported Agriculture membership and we started a small consumer-cooperative called TAQWA (from the Arabic, very loosely meaning "consciousness of God" in the Muslim faith). TAQWA purchases meat from local farmers that is humanely raised, on pasture, organic, slaughtered in the true spirit of Islamic dietary law, and brought directly to the market at the lowest possible cost. It also seeks to provide a living wage to the farmer and to all other humans involved in the processing chain. In other words, we bring in high quality agricultural products in ways that push more of the food dollar back down the value chain toward the farmer, without being cruel to the guys at the locker facility. We love farmers. We don't want to underpay them or poi-son them. We think the religious community should be interested in that.

TAQWA is a licensed meat broker. In our offices, tacked up to the wall, is our Illinois Department of Agriculture meat broker's license. We think this is funny. I don't remember meat broker day in seminary. Maybe I was sick.

I haven't had to do anything like putting a sheep in my car to take to slaughter, but I've come close. We participated in the official TAQWA lamb farm tour a few years back, during a big hoof-and-mouth scare, and we all had to put plastic booties over our shoes, then take them off as we left one farm, tossing them into a heavy-duty plastic garbage bag. At the next farm, we had to do it again, with fresh booties. I am wearing a pair of plastic booties over my running shoes in the photo from that day. I like the sheer, dumb absurdity of it. It seems like the right image for my own general lack of preparation for where I end up.

Clearly, it's not as if nothing has ever gone wrong. People have shown up at our meetings with heavy agendas of their own, and have taken advantage of the presence of an audience to do whatever business they came to do. Sometimes that is merely awkward, and sometimes it is downright unpleasant, but it hardly ever kills you. It's taught us to be clearer about our own agendas and a little tighter about the way we manage our events. We aren't quite so carefree about that sort of thing as we were when we started. It's not that we mind people having agendas that are different from our own — that's what makes the world go 'round — it's that we aren't here to create an audience for people who couldn't create one for themselves. We owe the people who support us a more direct relationship between what we expect to happen at our events and what actually does.

But I would have to say that the moments when someone took advantage, or spoke unkindly, or completely misinterpreted our intentions, have been very rare. They are painful when they've occurred, but happen so seldom that they hardly bear mentioning. We don't avoid conflict — we're perfectly happy to say challenging things, such as that capitalism is a problem when it comes to the environment. And we say other things that rub against the popular culture. Our faiths tell us to say those things; they tell us that the things that are most important are not accumulation of wealth, or the latest gadgetry, but love, compassion, respect and community. Expressed that way, our countercultural messages are hard to argue with. The thing is, most human beings know that the love they give and receive is much more important in the grand scheme of things than the kind of car they drive. We just need to be reminded occasionally.

Since I started this work I've driven probably 150,000 miles in the six-county area. I've showed up for meetings in snowstorms to find that no one came. I've planted all kinds of flowers, had some of the oddest members of the wide religious family offer blessings at events, gotten rained on any number of times, spent time on farms (in plastic booties), carried frozen chickens up stairs and opened up farmers markets at six in the morning.

I've witnessed a fire ceremony at a Zoroastrian temple, and found myself eating the traditional Zoroastrian sweets (shaped like a flower for the spring holiday), on a train to our state capitol, with Catholics, Unitarians, Lutherans and Zoroastrians heading down together to lobby on some environmental bills. Watching people who just met at the train station for the first time find delight in knowing each other, and making common purpose in our desire to leave the world better than we found it — it's a tight little miracle, the sort that has happened over and over in the last nine years. The humor and absurdity of so many moments make the miracles even sweeter.

If I've learned anything from this experiment in putting myself in the care of others in order to accomplish something dear to me, and of unknown importance to them, it's that our world is better than it appears in the media. I have learned this, and I have learned that our expectations will most often be met, so it's as well to have high ones for myself and for others, to be kind, and expect that others will be kind also. We living things and the earth have all turned out to be more resilient than we had any right to hope.

I really believe that the great decision of my generation is whether or not we will address global warming and the impact of humanity on this planet forthrightly, honestly, and with love for future generations. I am seeing people of all faiths drawn to the issue and ready to act. They act for the very survival of humans on earth and for a more awake and compassionate relationship between our species and the life that surrounds us. It may come in time, and it may not. But if we hold ourselves accountable to the words of love that all our faiths proclaim, we cannot do less than try. And just don't ever lose your sense of humor.

7

THE REV. WOODY BARTLETT
EPISCOPAL PRIEST (RETIRED)
ATLANTA, GEORGIA

# The Road to Green

"I stood there in tears, as St. Paul must have stood on
the Damascus road centuries ago. I had known in some
dull-witted way that we were harming our environment
in dangerous ways. But this? This was much
more than I had imagined."

Twenty years ago, I was in San Diego for a conference. I arrived a day early to attend a planning meeting, but try as I might, I couldn't find the meeting. As it turned out, the meeting and the conference were not the real reasons I was there. I was really there to start down a road that would change my life in unexpected ways.

So there I was in San Diego with a free day. What do you do with a free day in San Diego? You go to the zoo, of course.

I'd never been to that zoo before. It's a beautiful place, with many exotic creatures exhibited in their natural habitats. There are just a few cages and bars, with humans gathered around the animals like so many honeybees gathered around the first blossoms of spring.

As I wandered along the pathways, my curiosity was piqued by a red triangle with a white "E" in it at the top right corner of many of the exhibit markers. Looking at my guidebook, I was startled to find that the "E" meant "Endangered." Also alongside each of these exhibits was an explanation of how and why that particular species was so vulnerable; nearly all described the presence of humans as the prime cause. The red triangle started looking more blood-red to me. At the thought of the loss of so many gorgeous examples of God's creative exuberance, my eyes misted and the beauty of the spring day took on a more melancholy hue.

Finishing the tour of the zoo in the early afternoon, I went across the park to the Natural History Museum. It had the usual array of dinosaur bones and stuffed raccoons; but in one corner was a special display on extinction. With the red triangles in mind I headed straight there. Again were chronicled the numbers of species that were becoming extinct in our day. It was a litany that was quickly becoming familiar. The exhibit again pointed to the influence of man, *Homo sapiens,* as the cause of 99 percent of the extinctions!

Many of the creatures I saw at the zoo were also mentioned here. Even the Laplanders from the Arctic regions of Scandinavia and Russia were in the display. They are an endangered people because the fallout from the Chernobyl disaster has poisoned the reindeer — a staple of the Lapp diet — and so now the Lapps are at risk of permanent DNA damage and, ultimately, extinction. Things really got visceral then.

When I reached the end of the exhibit I faced one last chart whose message came crashing in on me:

*Rates of Extinction*

Before Man – I species per 1000 years
During the age of the dinosaurs – 100 species per year
At the present time – 1000 species per year
At the present rate – in 20 years – several species per hour
When humanity?

I was stunned at what I was seeing. We are in a period of extinction that is much, much harsher than that which had once wiped the mighty dinosaurs off the face of the Earth. At that time, 65 million years ago, up to 90 percent of the existing species, had disappeared. If it happened to them, it could surely happen to us. I became haunted by the image of a cage at the zoo with humans milling around in it. The marker would say *"Homo sapiens"* and it would have a red triangle with an E in the middle – Endangered!

I stood there in tears, as St. Paul must have stood on the Damascus road centuries ago. I had known in some dull-witted way that we were harming our environment in dangerous ways. But this? This was much more than I had imagined. I lurched for the exit but encountered one last sign:

*If all the beasts were gone, men would die from great loneliness of spirit, for whatever happens to the beasts happens to the man. All things are connected. Whatever befalls the Earth befalls the sons of the Earth.*

Chief Seattle
to the President of the US, 1855

Standing there, all I could do was picture a great crash of life carrying me and my kind to destruction. I thought of my family, my friends and my city. I thought of my faith. If Christ came to save us, then wasn't this what salvation should be about? But all my theology thus far concerned *personal* salvation; it seemed to have no relation to the extinction of the entire human species. What made a species live and what brought it to extinction? Did the life and message of Jesus relate to this issue at all? I had no idea.

I gathered myself and mumbled an earnest prayer; then I did what any self-respecting clergyman would do: I went to the bookstore and bought a book — on extinction. It was fascinating and I had finished it by the end of the conference. When I got back home, I devoured other books by the same author. My wife, Carol, and I formed a small group that got together and wrestled with theology, slowly figuring out what we believed as Christians in the context of the whole community of life, not just our own smaller, human community.

Two years later, I took the only sabbatical I had during my whole ministry and spent it exploring ecological issues. I went to several conferences and visited many environmental programs across the country. By the end of the sabbatical I had started writing in order to get my thoughts organized. Thirteen years later that inchoate thinking finally appeared in a book, *Living By Surprise: A Christian Response to the Ecological Crisis*, published in 2003 by Paulist Press.

Carol and I tried several different avenues to turn our growing convictions to more practical ends. We tried organizing the Episcopal Church with some degree of success, but we were met with a considerable degree of apathy. There were a number of interested lay people, but very few clergy could fit this issue into their already over-crowded lives. Environmental concerns were not on many people's agendas in those days. And besides, our efforts had little focus.

Later we formed a "consulting" group to work with individual churches. That effort had even less success as we still could find few takers. Finally in 2001, after my retirement, we were asked to administer a conference on air pollution. It turned out to be a fairly successful event with the side benefit that we finally found our focus: air pollution and global warming, both important drivers in species loss as well as threats to human health.

In mid-2002 we heard that our local power company, Georgia Power, would be offering a "green energy" option to their customers. This meant that they would provide electricity generated from non-polluting sources, an answer to both air pollution and global warming. We saw in this a perfect opportunity for churches to be a part of the solution. Talking to a friend who ran a local environmental organization on clean air, someone mentioned the Rev. Sally Bingham and the Interfaith Power and Light movement. We called her. She said that if we formed a steering committee, she would come and help us get started. She did, and Georgia Interfaith Power and Light was born. Now, five years later, we have two full time staff people, a budget of $125,000 and close to 150 participating congregations.

Our first task after kickoff was to file an official intervention into the green energy case being presented by Georgia Power Company to the Georgia Public Service Commission. In a utility-regulated state like Georgia, everything relating to the generation and use of energy gets worked out in a series of public hearings and discussions. The result is an order from the Commission regulating that particular issue. We were small and new but we had an official seat at the table! We made a few contributions but much of that early effort went to learning the rather arcane language of kilowatts, energy and sustainability. However, we did add to the final order an affordable way for congregations to purchase green energy. But, beyond some vague promises from Georgia Power, we were unsuccessful in getting Georgia Power to submit their new product for certification by an independent third party agency. Certification is the Good Housekeeping Seal of Approval for renewable energy. It guarantees that the product is what it is purported to be and that its clean air attributes are properly used. We felt that we should not risk our growing public credibility by actively promoting a product without this certification.

Four years later and somewhat out of the blue, as part of another Georgia Power case settlement, we got Georgia Power to agree to apply for certification. They did, and it was granted. So now, with the help of some volunteer marketing people, we are ramping up to promote the purchase of green energy to our constituency.

Despite our struggle with Georgia Power, our IPL chapter was moving ahead. In those beginning days, the steering committee agreed that we wanted to promote energy efficiency for electricity users as well as to encourage the generation of energy from clean, green sources. The easiest place to start on efficiency was to encourage the use of compact fluorescent light bulbs (CFLs). We received a gift of $3,000 to equip ourselves with a supply of bulbs, found a wonderful wholesaler, and started having bulb sales in congregations. Our garage became the warehouse for the bulbs. It was sometimes a logistics nightmare as a huge 18-wheeler would drive up to our house and unload a pallet of bulbs. But we soldiered on.

We developed literature that showed how a CFL uses only about one-quarter of the energy that an incandescent bulb does to give the same light. We developed a chart showing that, even though CFLs cost more at first, over their extended lifetimes, a user would save $35.74, or 71 percent, per bulb.

Our greatest bulb sale coup happened when we were given a demonstration electric meter that had been used by a major Atlanta corporation as they switched their office to CFLs. It was made of a standard electric meter with two regular light bulb sockets mounted on top. You could put a 60 Watt incandescent bulb in one socket and a 13 Watt CFL in the other, turn each one on and watch the difference as the meter wheel spun around – the incandescent bulb caused it to spin quickly and the CFL made it spin slowly, while they each produced the same amount of light. People were amazed as they watched and were instantly sold on CFLs as a way to save money. We were preventing harmful emissions into the atmosphere one CFL at a time. And, perhaps even more significantly, we noticed that people were starting to gear up for a bigger push that would soon have to come to adequately respond to climate change.

There was one person on the steering committee who decided to put a distinctively Jewish twist on the sale of CFLs. He and another man at his synagogue developed a Hanukkah kit called *One for Each Night: A Hanukkah Study Guide for a Brighter Future*. It consists of eight CFLs and a study guide. Each night of Hanukkah, the user lights a traditional candle and then swaps an old light bulb for a new CFL. The study guide offers a meditation for each night on the environmental benefits of using CFLs. And at the top of each page is a Jewish light bulb joke — of course! They came up with their jokes through a competition in the synagogue and they are quite funny, although some are clearly for insiders and fly way over my head.

Traditionally, during the season of Hanukkah the Jewish people give gifts wrapped in festive cloth bags. So our Hanukkah kits were wrapped in cloth bags. As the idea caught on, we found ourselves shopping for bolts of cloth with a Hanukkah theme, setting up "sewing circles" to cut and sew the bags and having committees assemble the kits. It became our own little cottage industry.

Then we expanded the concept and created an Advent kit for Christians. This project had a bit less of an environmental impact since there were only five bulbs instead of eight — the four Sundays in Advent plus the Christ candle for Christmas Eve. Called *Preparing for a New Light: Caring for God's Creation During Advent*, this study guide is patterned on the Hanukkah guide and, it too offers light bulb jokes for different denominations. Now these I get! How many Episcopalians does it take to change a light bulb? Answer: Ten. One to change the bulb, and nine to say how much better they liked the old one.

Efficiency through the installation of CFLs was our theme. But we felt a nagging concern that poor people couldn't afford both the up-front cost of CFLs along with the continuing and rising cost of power. And the poor were often the ones most affected by the negative environmental impacts of coal-fired power generation because they tend to live near where those plants operate, receiving the direct impacts of the pollution generated. What to do?

I spoke to one of my old activist friends in the African American community, Joe Beasley. Joe coordinates poverty ministries in a large African American church, Antioch Baptist Church, North. They have active ministries to the poor and are at the forefront of most any social movement happening.

As we talked, Joe mentioned that they had an ongoing relationship with a large public housing project right across the street from the church. Perhaps we could swap out new CFLs for old incandescent bulbs in that complex. He called the president of the tenants association and she told us she thought it was a workable idea. We went to see the staff at the Atlanta Housing Authority and they thought it was useful also. Everywhere we turned, people were eager to pitch in: We spoke to the efficiency people at Georgia Power and they agreed to donate the light bulbs for the effort. We talked to the leaders in the Saturday morning Men's Prayer Breakfast and they were happy to participate. We talked to the management company in the housing project and they were willing to help. They divided the complex into areas and assigned a maintenance worker to each area, many of whom came from different complexes and were volunteering their time.

So one Saturday morning in November 2006, we gathered at Antioch for the regular prayer breakfast, sang some hymns, said some prayers, heard a bit of inspired preaching and got ourselves organized. At 10 o'clock, 50 of us went across the street where we were met by 15 or 20 maintenance workers who would lead teams throughout the project. We gathered around the huge stack of boxes containing the CFLs that had been delivered by Georgia Power, split into teams and headed out. The maintenance worker in each team would knock on a door, shout, "Maintenance!" and if there was no answer, he or she would use a passkey to enter the apartment. Then we would climb on chairs or ladders, unscrew the old bulbs and put in brand new CFLs. Old bulbs and empty boxes were heaped into plastic bags. A superintendent in a golf cart continually cruised through the complex, picking up the sacks and keeping the supply of new bulbs flowing.

We had lively conversations with residents and only a few broken bulbs. By one o'clock, as we retreated back to Antioch for a tasty fried chicken lunch, we had replaced some 3,500 light bulbs. Over the expected lifetime of those CFLs, we had saved almost 1,300 tons of $CO_2$ from the atmosphere and some $140,000 in electricity costs. It was a great day.

We're down the road to green a bit now. We're still pushing CFLs, but now through IPL's national shopping cart. We're also showing educational videos, doing congregational energy audits and giving matching grants for energy improvements – and we plan to branch out into solar energy. It's a wonderful road, and it's getting greener and greener.

## 8

MOHAMAD A. CHAKAKI
MUSLIM ENVIRONMENTAL ACTIVIST AND EDUCATOR
WASHINGTON, DC

# Our True Nature:
## The Islamic Concept of Fitra and Healing the Connection to the Child Within

"Before our children are old enough to understand or be
taught the meaning of ritual, they can learn a deep spirituality,
and receive lessons that will last them a lifetime, from the
natural world. Instead, we cut our children and ourselves
off from nature, not allowing it to impress its wisdom
upon us in its subtle yet lasting way."

❧

They're beaming, literally glowing. I can feel it, their warmth and their energy. It fills the room and it's uplifting. I'm happy to see them, but they're happier to see me. I'm smiling, almost as wide as they are. I reach out to touch them, just to make sure this is real. This is real. They're real — little angels, but real. I pat them on their little heads and shake their little hands. These are my children, my students. I don't see them often enough, but when I do see them I'm happy and consider myself blessed. Then I realize, I saw these same children yesterday. They were glowing, happy and smiling, but somehow I didn't notice it yesterday. Why didn't I notice it?

I consult and teach at two schools in the Washington, DC, area. They are very different schools, but in many ways very much the same. The first is a small, community-based school that began as a home schooling co-op for pre-school-aged children. That first crop of students is now about to enter high school, with a small but steady number of children coming up through the grades behind them.

The second is a school for youth offenders, a detention and rehabilitation center for high-school-age boys. It was on a week when, on back-to-back days, I went from this detention center for young men to a homey classroom of third and fourth graders, did the similarities between both schools dawn on me, the similarities between both sets of students — all children within, despite the differences on the outside.

I remember walking into the elementary office one Friday morning and asking the administrators (mothers of the children at the school) if everyone and everything was OK. With the students and the school, that is. It's the question I ask whenever I check in at the detention center: Any incidents? Any fights? Anybody released a short while ago only to be back in again for something else? How are the teachers? Is everyone and everything OK?

It seemed like a strange question at the time, but I spent the day before at what was basically a jail for teenagers. The students there are tough. They're hard to reach and, though I hate to admit it, often hard to love. But I realized, over the course of a few weeks working with them, that this was all a shell. These were only layers of negativity, violence and abuse that came from growing up in broken families and bad neighborhoods.

I love children, for many reasons. They make me smile and laugh. They keep me honest. They bring brightness and blessings into my life. That day, though, that Friday morning in the elementary classroom, I connected these little ones to the young offenders at the detention center. They are also children. Beneath that tough "gangsta" exterior and all those layers of negativity, even the most hardened youth offenders are just as fresh and as present as any child.

This freshness and presence does not end with children. It extends to everybody. Everyone has a child inside, hidden behind the layers of what life has thrown at us and we have not shed. That is one of the secrets truths about children and interacting with them regularly. Our children remind us of what it is like to be a child again. Namely, what it means to be present, relatively unguarded, happy and whole. In a word, rejuvenated — literally, young again.

We are born close to this wholeness. The Qur'an states that God is the cleaver of heaven and earth. In the same way, our earthly existence is also cleaved from a heavenly one. God cleaves us from our primordial state of oneness, wholeness and completeness into individual human beings. This is our *fitra*, our true nature. The root word of *fitra* in Arabic (*fa-ta-ra*) is a verb that means "to cleave."

Children are the closest to their *fitra*. As we grow older, how-ever, we begin to forget. This is called *ghafla*, literally a state of unconsciousness or sleep. Children, then, are alive and awake. They remind us of this conscious state of being in the world.

To be sure, there are many things in this world that remind us of our *fitra*. The Qur'an calls these signposts on the path of our lives *ayaat*, which literally means "signs." There are signs on the horizon and signs within our selves, a world without and a world within. There are also signs in the Qur'an, and the verses therein are also referred to as *ayaat*. Thus, there is a Book of Scripture (i.e., the Qur'an) and a metaphorical Book of Nature (i.e., the natural world).

Children, in touch with both their inner and outer worlds in an open and unguarded way, are also signs. The remind us what it means to be open, honest and loving toward one another, and enchanted and in awe of the world around us. This, again, is *fitra*.

Second to the Qur'an, the most important source of Islamic law, faith and spirituality, is the Prophet Muhammad. His example, in words and deeds, are referred to as the *sunnah*. There are two aspects of the Prophet Muhammad's life that are relevant to our discussion: his childhood connection to the natural world and the depth of his spirituality (if that can be fathomed at all) as a man; indeed, this is also the pinnacle of Islamic spirituality.

These two aspects of the Prophet Muhammad's life are by no means unrelated. In fact, that is part of the argument that Tariq Ramadan (a renowned European-Muslim thinker) makes in his recent biography of the Prophet Muhammad, *In the Footsteps of the Prophet: Lessons from the Life of Muhammad*. This is what Ramadan has to say:

*In the first years of the Prophet's life he developed a specific relation-ship with nature that remained constant throughout his mission. ...This relationship with nature was so present in the Prophet's life from his earliest childhood that one can easily come to the conclusion that liv-ing close to nature, observing, understanding, and respecting it, is an imperative of deep faith.*

As was the wont of the people in Mecca, children (infants, really) were sent out to live with Bedouin tribes in the deserts sur-rounding the city. It was thought that this would be a healthier, more invigorating environment than the city of Mecca. Living among the Bedouins, preservers of the highest forms of Arab lan-guage and customs, would also instill the values of Arab culture in the children. The Prophet Muhammad spent his earliest years with the tribe of Bani Sa'ad. He had lost his father before he was born and was being cared for by his mother and grandfather.

Muhammad would move back to Mecca after his mother's death and, upon the death of his grandfather, come under the care of his uncle Abu Talib. The young Muhammad, now in middle childhood, spent his days tending to his uncle's sheep in the hills surrounding Mecca. This is how Ramadan interprets this aspect of the Prophet Muhammad's early life:

*Thus, God decided to expose His Prophet, from his earliest childhood, to the natural lessons of creation, conceived as a school where the mind gradually apprehends signs and meaning. Far removed from the formal-ism of soulless religious rituals, this sort of education, in and through its closeness to nature, fosters a relationship to the divine based on con-templation and depth that will later make it possible, in a second phase of spiritual education, to understand the meaning, form, and objectives of religious ritual.*

Ramadan goes on to explain how we, in our modern disconnection from nature, are inverting the order of this Prophetic example, or *sunnah*. Before our children are old enough to understand or be taught the meaning of ritual, they can learn a deep spirituality, and receive lessons that will last them a lifetime, from the natural world. Instead, we cut our children and ourselves off from nature, not allowing it to impress its wisdom upon us in its subtle yet lasting way.

Tariq Ramadan ends his discussion of nature and spirituality with a warning: "This delusion," he writes, "has serious consequences since it leads to draining religious teaching of its spiritual substance, which actually ought to be its heart." Formal religion without a spirituality that is grounded in a deep connection to the world around us (and I believe that this is what empathy really is, for others and for nature) is heartless. That is dangerous.

I would like to turn back to our children's disconnection from nature for a moment. Nowhere has this phenomenon been more clearly elucidated than in Richard Louv's recent book, *Last Child Left in the Woods: Saving Our Children from Nature Deficit Disorder*. His phrase, "nature deficit disorder," speaks volumes. But I would like to focus on a single, but telling, aspect of Louv's argument:

Early on in the book, Louv characterizes a number of things that disconnect the current generation of children from nature. One of these is a "hyper-intellectualization" of animals. In other words, before many of our children have ever interacted with an animal (especially a wild animal) and communed with it as another creature or living, breathing being, they have studied animals only in terms of atoms, molecules, organelles, cells, tissues, organs, systems, organisms or, worse yet, they've dissected them. This too is an inversion of a natural order of sorts. It paves they way for further disconnection in later years and for a lack of empathy that is reflected in our fear of and cruelty toward animals, specifically, and the natural world in general – including other people.

While this may seem far afield from our discussion of the Prophet Muhammad and spirituality, it is not. For what characterizes the Prophet's spirituality is precisely a deep connection to the world around him, be that the earth, plants, animals or other people.

*Tasbih,* from the root verb *"sa-ba-ha"* in Arabic, meaning "to swim" or "be immersed in," is how creation recognizes and meditates upon the all-encompassing presence of the Creator. In fact, at the height of spiritual progress in Islam, humans have had the ability to hear and understand creation's *tasbih,* to say nothing of discoursing with the creatures. This is also reflected in the teachings of Prophet Muhammad and so many other prophets and saints. The Qur'an is clear on how very few of us can comprehend this meditative state:

> *The Night Journey (17:44): The seven heavens and the earth, and all beings therein, declare His glory* (tasbih)*: there is not a thing but celebrates* (tasbih) *His praise; And yet ye understand not how they declare His glory* (tasbih)*! Verily He is Oft-Forbearing, Most Forgiving!*

There are a number of instances in the Prophet Muhammad's adult life when his connection to the natural world is made manifest by the dialogue he enters into with certain creatures. These include calming the trembling Mountain of Hira outside of Mecca as he and his companions were walking upon it, talking to the crescent moon at its birth and the dawning of a new lunar month, listening to a camel that complained to him of ill treatment by its owner and, finally, hugging and consoling a tree.

This last image, the Prophet Muhammad hugging a tree, is certainly worth more attention. The text of a rigorously authenticated tradition (*hadith sahih*) of the Prophet gives us the detail:

> *Narrated by Jabir bin ʿAbdullah (a companion of the Prophet Muhammad): The Prophet used to stand by a tree or a date-palm on Friday. Then an Ansari (a native of Medina) woman or man said, "O Messenger of God! Shall we make a pulpit for you?" He replied, "If you wish." So they made a pulpit for him and when it was Friday, he proceeded towards the pulpit (to deliver the sermon). The date-palm cried like a child! The Prophet descended (the pulpit) and embraced it while it continued moaning like a child being consoled. The Prophet said, "It was crying for (missing) what it used to hear of religious knowledge given near to it."* Sahih al-Bukhari; Vol. 4, Book 56, Num. 784

In another narration, the Prophet Muhammad not only hugs the tree trunk, but also speaks to it. Muslims cannot deny the fact that their prophet spoke to plants, animals and even inanimate creatures. But how do we interpret such events? Where do we place them in our modern cosmology or worldview? Do they have a place in our modern understanding of the universe?

Such stories speak volumes about how deep our connection to nature could be, and about the ethic and empathy that it should inspire in us — to say nothing of the enchantment, wonder and awe that we should have with, in and of, nature. Again, this is the way of children and a perspective closer to our *fitra*. The Prophet Muhammad, a model for Muslim life in his words and deeds, was child-like in his closeness to his *fitra*. This is why he was also so close to children, as Tariq Ramadan so touchingly explains:

*The Messenger loved children, with their innocence, gentleness and ability to be present in the moment. Close to God, close to his own heart, he remained attentive to those who primarily understood the heart's language. He kissed them, carried them on his shoulders, and played with them, reaching toward their innocence, which is in its essence the expression of a permanent prayer to God... The Messenger moreover, drew from children his sense of play and innocence; from them he learned to look at people and the world around him with wonder.*

There are children in all of us. Healing the connection to ourselves, to the children within, is the first step to healing our connection to those around us (family, friends, community and society) and to the world around us (the earth or natural world), and vice versa. For once this healing begins, it flows back and forth and reinforces itself. The first step, however, is to heal ourselves; to find and reconnect to that child within that is still in awe of the world, and the mystery, wonder and enchantment to be found therein.

⁂

"And God is more knowledgeable," is the phrase Muslims traditionally use to end their writing. Beyond that, I am grateful to Afeefa Syeed, Sophia Kizilbash, Tarek Elgawhary and the children, whose wisdom and experience informed and inspired the concepts in this chapter. Any shortcomings, however, are my own.

## 9

Dr. Joel Hunter
Senior Pastor, Northland Church
Orlando, Florida

# Loving Your Neighbor
## (and embracing conflict)

"My work to help people take better care of the environment has taught me a few things about myself and the ministry in general. First, you never really know how conflict avoidant you are until you get into one of these 'hotly debated' issues."

ॐ

**M**y friends are always getting me in trouble.

Three years ago Richard Cizik and Jim Ball asked me to sign on to a statement called the Evangelical Climate Initiative. I didn't know Jim well then, but I had worked with Richard in my capacity as a board member of the National Association of Evangelicals. I esteemed both of these national leaders as respected colleagues.

My first thought was, "Huh? There's a problem with the environment?" Of course, I knew all about pollution. I had grown up in Ohio where at one time the Cuyahoga River was so polluted it caught on fire (they've cleaned it up since so you can't roast marshmallows on top of the water anymore). But wait! They weren't just talking about regular old don't-pour-car-oil-on-the-ground pollution; they were talking about air pollution so bad that it was affecting the climate. "Global Warming" they called it.

I've got to be honest, it sounded like the old "snipe hunt" practical joke where people around you talk so seriously about these animals you've never heard of, then take you out at night to hunt for them, and you find yourself alone in the dark with your "friends" laughing so hard they're holding their sides.

Yet I knew these guys weren't the snipe-hunt types. So I began to investigate all I could find about this new phenomenon. I read books like Tim Flannery's *The Weathermakers* and actual portions of the Intergovernmental Panel on Climate Change reports. I also read some of the material of the skeptics, like Fred Singer (University of Virginia) and Richard Lindzen (MIT). As a non-scientist simply trying to understand a reasonable portion of the evidence, I was shocked at what I had not even considered up to that time. I decided I believed the broad consensus of scientific findings represented best by the Intergovernmental Panel on Climate Change. Then I had to decide how to react.

To a follower of Christ, any evidence of a problem that can harm people quickly presents three questions: Can I do anything about this? If I can help, what is the right thing to do? Since every attempt to do right has unintended consequences, what is the wise way to do the right thing?

I signed on to the statement. I even participated in a nationally aired commercial urging action on global warming. But as a pastor, taking those actions was just the shot pistol going off at the beginning of a marathon.

## THE NEGATIVE RESPONSES

As a clip of the national commercial made it onto prime time news, many of my congregation heard about this relatively new emphasis in my involvement. The response was swift from some. They were not angry at me – OK, a few were furious, but most were just trying to protect me:

"Pastor, don't you know this is a dangerous hoax? Have you read Michael Crichton's *State of Fear*? This could end up embarrassing you, the church, and even the cause of Christ! Please reconsider!"

Yes, for every action, there is an equal and opposite reaction. And just as I meant well by my advocacy, they meant well by their resistance.

As time went on, the responses from some quarters of the larger church got meaner. I was being accused of being a tool of the devil to divert the church from its true calling. I was being accused of the kind of ignorance or naiveté that would *harm* the poor rather then help them. My friends and fellow advocates for Biblical stewardship of the earth were being painted as alarmist extremists, more interested in fear than sense. I was getting irritated, but then I remembered some very important facts.

## The Role of Debate

As a history and government major in my undergraduate work, I knew some of the characteristics we have as a people. In our country (and hence in our churches), we have developed a culture of debate. It's in the DNA of our democracy and promoted by the checks and balances of our governmental structure. Debate is how we make progress in science, philosophy and solution-finding. Debate is also how we have learned how to best express our faith positions with reasoned, as well as passionate, actions. It is in our history and in our entertainment. But as to the latter category, much of the debate has mutated into angry accusation.

Listening to the talk show hosts, it seemed as if you could not believe in global warming without at least being a disciple of Al Gore or an extreme tree-hugging earth worshipper. Conservatism became aligned with believing that anthropogenic climate change was a hoax, promoted by people who wanted government to take over our lives. So I was being accused by some conservative bloggers and a local talk show host as a "liberal dressed up in conservative clothing."

Likewise, on the more liberal side of the accusations, the skeptics of the skeptics said that those who questioned the scientific conclusions pertaining to climate change were knuckle-dragging Neanderthals who would deny the earth was round.

Meanwhile, I, along with practically every pastor in America, had congregations containing both believers in the majority science and skeptics claiming there was no scientific consensus on climate change or its causes. To avoid the risk of dividing the congregation, most pastors chose to avoid the issue altogether. I was not that cautious, but I had to decide how to gather support for Creation

Care most wisely within my own affinity group: evangelical Christians.

## Bible Basics

For an evangelical pastor who believes that the Bible reveals the Person and will of God, an approach to solving any problem in life must be linked to an understanding of scriptures. For me, involvement in Creation Care (that's what we evangelicals like to call environmental stewardship) was very simple. In my life, it would be focused on three Biblical passages:

1. Genesis 2:15 relays the first job man ever received from God: "Then the Lord God took the man and put him into the Garden of Eden to cultivate it and keep it." The Hebrew words for "cultivate and keep" are roughly translated by the words you can see on the side of many police cars: "to serve and protect." Therefore, protection of the earth from that which could ruin its productivity is a direct order from God.

2. Luke 10:30-37 communicates a command from Jesus to help people who happen to be in need, as we have the occasion and the resources to do so. In the story of the Good Samaritan, Jesus tells of a hurting person helped by someone who did not know him. He then orders everyone who will listen to him, "Go and do the same." For me, it is simply a directive from my Lord to do what I can with what I have, wherever I am, to help with the problems that plague people. In this story, a neighbor is defined as someone who will help those in need.

3. In Matthew 22:37-39, loving God with our whole heart is linked with this command, "you shall love your neighbor as

you love yourself." In this passage not only is caring about our neighbor central, but the justice principle of "as you love yourself" advances our neighbor's well-being to be on par with our own.

In my life as a pastor, environmental care has never originated as a political stance. Environmental stewardship is a direct Biblical and moral mandate that has everything to do with loving God and neighbor. True, because I seek consistency, I have become a voice that speaks these values into public policy, but that is only after personal and church action.

## Many People, One Cause

In getting involved in the global challenge of environmental degradation, what has been of great benefit to me as a pastor is the chance to work with so many people that I would never ordinarily have met. Invitations to collaborate from outside as well as inside my church have proven to be invaluable. New relationships have come in a variety of ways:

I have relished being invited to conferences with like-minded believers and non-believers as well. This issue has been an incredible catalyst for connecting with leaders and organizations that have a common concern for life. Many times a Christian leader gets stuck within the "church world," and more specifically his or her own church. When I can meet other Christians in non-Christian organizations, it connects me in ways I could never have been linked before. After one of my talks, a member of the Sierra Club whispered, "There are lots of Christians in this Club!" At that same event, I was on the dais with John Podesta (President Clinton's former Chief of Staff), a UN official, and the international president of Friends of the Earth. In other events I have met Prince Charles, senators, congressmen, international Christian leaders such as Bishop James Jones of Liverpool and author N.T. Wright, and scientists such as E.O. Wilson and James Hanson. All of us together are concerned about this issue. With many, I have formed at least a cordial relationship, and I am open to further conversations.

I also got connected with Rev. Sally Bingham and Interfaith Power and Light. She invited a broad range of religious leaders to San Francisco. There were only about twelve of us, but we represented large and varied constituencies – from the Presiding Bishop of the Episcopal Church to the President of the Islamic Society of North America. It felt a little weird even to be in that group, and to add to the surreal experience, we stayed in a "green" hotel that had a fire alarm glitch. Now, those who care for the earth aren't known for our beauty in the first place, but standing on the street at 3 o'clock in the morning...yikes!

I have been surprised at the bridge this issue has built with people of the younger generations. A result of speaking out on the dangers of climate change has been a new conversation with people my kids' age. I was born in 1948, so my natural following is more middle age. But after a college newspaper did an interview, I could not believe my new "street cred." Yes, on this issue young and old stand together.

And the surprises continue: Much closer to home, I have been delighted to work with people in my own congregation that I never would have known otherwise. After we showed the movie *The Great Warming* in our church, about a dozen people out of the 400 who attended were moved to take on the responsibility to advance Creation Care in and for our church. They have done an incredible job. They have sorted a week's worth of trash to identify waste patterns for recycling and reducing. They have produced a 140-page audit for our church on everything from energy usage to solid-waste management to landscaping/watering. We are using the audit as a benchmark and strategy for measuring our progress toward lowering our carbon footprint. Additionally, they organized a Creation Care Weekend in which 30 vendors came to the church and set up displays of environmentally friendly products that our congregation could browse through after worship. And as a result of their vision, we hosted a Creation Care Conference in which national and local leaders (including a Rabbi and an Imam) taught other local leaders about how to develop congregational participation in this effort.

All of this experience has connected me to parts of our community and state that I would not normally have been called upon to reach. One day, Orange County Mayor, Rich Crotty, phoned me and said, in essence, "I'm all for becoming environmentally friendly at a metropolitan level. With the global warming issue, I'm thinking that even if we are wrong, the worst we can do is improve the environment." So the Mayor is turning the county "green." and our Governor, Charlie Crist, is taking after Arnold Schwarzenegger (except for that whole muscle thing) when it comes to the environment. I am now able to be active in the public square, not only my congregation, because of this one common cause.

Finally, do you know the unanticipated benefit of taking care of the environment? You get to work with so many great and compassionate people that you have a chance to partner on other projects as well. Many of those I meet at environmental events are also active in finding solutions to poverty, pandemic disease (such as AIDS), justice issues, etc.

## NEW LESSONS

I became a pastor because I wanted to help people get closer to God. My work to help people take better care of the environment has taught me a few things about myself and the ministry in general.

First, you never really know how conflict avoidant you are until you get into one of these "hotly debated" issues. Yes, in the evangelical church the catalytic issue to prompt environmental care, global warming, is still hotly debated. In fact, I was talking with a ministry leader the other day who goes to my church. He was telling me that my name was getting kicked around a bit in some ministry circles because I'm taking on these "liberal issues." He said that he was going to stick with me even though he flatly announced, "I don't believe in global warming." Now, here was a friend, a man with whom I had cooperated in ministry, signaling to me that his closeness to me might be on thin ice — which is not good in a warming climate.

Yet if friendships in church are built on issue agreement rather than a deep kinship in Christ, they are not going to last very long. There is no need for me to avoid the inevitable conflict that comes with trying to do the right thing, as long as I can give others the freedom to believe or walk in a different direction. I just need to keep focusing on Creation Care as a way to honor the Creator. Only that emphasis will accomplish my original reason for getting into ministry.

Second, since I am a results-oriented kind of guy, I take great comfort in the fact that there are relational, practical, financial, as well as spiritual, benefits in doing the right thing. Being a part of a broader circle of colleagues is a means of making progress in multiple ways, in addition to improving my personal habits and my church's involvement. I can serve in advancing the environmental agenda of a wide variety of other organizations, from the First Green Bank of Florida, to Republicans for Interfaith Power and Light, to Republicans for Environmental Protection, to I Sky! And we all (for these benefits might be yours as well) can enjoy these new relationships while we are saving money and doing the right thing for God and His people.

## 10

RABBI DANIEL SWARTZ
TEMPLE HESED (REFORM)
SCRANTON, PA

# One-Night Stands vs. Sustainable Change

"[O]ne of our core 'environmental' values as people of faith is
that all of us, equally created in God's image, are Children of
the Creator and worth protecting from environmental disasters.
That means, of course, even those who disagree with us!"

❧

For most of my rabbinate I have served in organizations connected to hundreds of congregations, rather than in the pulpit
of one synagogue.

For a number of those years, I focused my efforts on inspiring
congregations to address climate change, and then helping to guide
them as they began taking action. At first my guidance was geared
towards the technical: what a compact fluorescent light (CFL) is
and the types available, how to find energy savings devices, how to
purchase "green" energy, and so forth. Gradually, however, I began

to realize that while energy-saving techniques for congregations usually resembled one another, each congregation faced its own problems with implementing them.

In one place, a significant donor to the congregation had tried CFLs in her home years before and objected to their color, so money could not be spent on them until the Pastor visited the donor in her home and demonstrated a variety of new bulbs until one finally met her approval. In another, the board member who had championed energy conservation was pushed off the board for unrelated reasons; unfortunately, the new board members associated energy conservation with the "fallen" board member and therefore didn't want to touch the issue. In each house of worship, people struggled toward carbon neutrality in different ways, facing different obstacles, specific to their denomination, their clergy, their history and their location. I could get things started, but long-term engagement had to be an inside job, not the result of outsiders, however inspiring or knowledgeable.

I went from congregation to congregation, leaving CFLs in my wake like an updated Johnny Appleseed; and like Johnny, I was usually not around to tend the saplings as they grew, because there were just too many places where I had been and still needed to go to. Over time, a more apt metaphor came to mind: I felt like a member of a band on tour, having a series of one-night stands. I did the exciting, glamorous work — speaking at a special service or giving a PowerPoint presentation to an eager audience — and then I whooshed off to the next stop. It was someone else's job to do the cleanup afterwards, and to harness the energy I had generated into sustainable efforts at energy conservation and faith-based activism.

All this came to head for me after a particularly good sermon at a large Unitarian Church. I outlined some of the principles faith communities can be guided by as they address climate change, such as, the goodness of God's creation, the long-term nature of religious covenants, the importance of tending first and foremost to the needs of the most vulnerable in our communities (human and non-human alike). There was applause as I concluded each section, and when I finished, I received a standing ovation. Since Jews don't clap at all, in my experience, let alone give standing ovations, it was a pretty heady moment for me. Afterwards, an eager young man came up to thank me and said, "Rabbi Swartz, your speech changed my life." I thought about that for a moment, and then replied, "That's a sweet thing to say, but it's not quite true. No single speech changes anyone's life. It can serve as a catalyst, but change is a long, hard process that you'll need to keep working at constantly." As soon as the words left my mouth, I realized that I too wanted to initiate a change in my life, to get back into congregational life, to build a sustainable relationship with one congregation over time, to try to slowly shape it into a model for other green congregations.

I've been back in the pulpit now for almost two years, and during that time I've learned a tremendous amount, not the least of which is that I still have lots to learn. But I'm already coming up with a new set of principles to guide my work as I seek depth over breadth. I know I will keep adding to the list as I keep learning, but for now, here are my first five:

## Kids are Key

Kids are key to sustainable success, for a variety of reasons. On a practical level, almost no religious institution thinks it is doing so well with its childhood education programs that it isn't willing to consider some improvements. Often, changes to children's curricula that address creation care in general and faith-based response to climate change in particular can take place more rapidly than almost anything else. For example, in my synagogue, in the time it took me to get nine energy-wasting exit signs replaced with energy-efficient LED signs, I was able to revamp the entire K-through-10 curriculum to include lessons about climate change at every level. As I made those changes, it became clear to me that children are not only more open to learning new things, but that they are also more willing to integrate these lessons into their basic world view. Thus, when the students were challenged to design a city based on Jewish values, one of the first things they did was to set aside space for a wind farm and plan neighborhoods around public transportation! This parallels a teaching in the early rabbinic work, *Avot de Rabbi Nathan*, section 24:

> *When you learn Torah as a youth, it is like ink written on new parchment. When you learn in your old age, it is like ink written on parchment that has been used and erased, used and erased. When you learn Torah as a youth, it is absorbed into your very blood and then never ceases to come forth from your mouth. When you learn Torah in old age, it is never absorbed into your blood.*

I hope — and expect — that these children will continue to hold true to these values as they grow. As Proverbs 22:6 teaches, "Train children in the way they should go, and when they are old they will not depart from it." What is also clear is that children are great agents of propaganda! I can't tell you how many times I've heard from parents, "Where do I buy those CFL things; my daughter won't stop talking about them," or "How do you like your Prius? My son insists that our next car needs to be a hybrid." Clearly, it is not just in the messianic vision of Isaiah (11:6) that "a little child shall lead them."

## EACH OF US IS – AND ISN'T – KEY

One of my all-time favorite Jewish quotes is the teaching of Rabbi Tarfon found in *Pirke Avot* (The Sayings of the Ancestors) 2:21: "It is not up to you to complete the task, but neither are you free to desist from it." Especially in our environmental work, it is easy to feel that unless we succeed at everything we do, the world will move toward destruction, while on the other hand we may feel that nothing we do makes any difference. Tarfon helps us navigate a course between these two poles. We are a needed part of the overall equation, but our efforts alone will not solve the problem. So, do not sit back thinking your part in the overall struggle is of no import; but also, do not act as if the weight of the whole movement is upon your shoulders alone. Only when we all work together, each of us valuing both our own efforts and those of others, will our actions eventually bear fruit.

## WELCOME DIFFERENCES OF OPINION

More and more, political "discussions" in America consist of ritual proclamations of one's own view and absolute condemnations of any dissenting views. In our houses of worship and study, we can and should do better. Even as we work passionately for the preservation of the future of our planet and our people, we need to show compassion by respecting those with opposing views. By welcoming them into the discussion, we stand a much better chance of breaking down obstacles that have kept them from understanding the importance of our climate change concerns. Moreover, hearing opposing views, far from weakening our arguments, should ultimately serve to strengthen them. The Talmud teaches that as "iron sharpens iron, so too do differences of opinion sharpen one another's mind." This teaching from *Sefer Hasidim*, a 13th century work, reminds us that sometimes even our most well considered opinions can be wrong (as hard as that may be to believe sometimes...). Thus, by listening to others, we have the ability to see our own mistakes not as defects but as opportunities to gain wisdom. Most importantly, one of our core "environmental" values as people of faith is that *all of us*, equally created in God's image, are Children of the Creator and worth protecting from environmental disasters. That means, of course, even those who disagree with us!

## "No" Just Means "Not Yet"

The famous environmental activist David Brower said that all environmental victories are temporary, while all such defeats are permanent. This attitude can sometimes be a great motivator, but it can also paralyze people and shut down any possibility of action. Especially within religious institutions, I prefer to think that when I get "no" for an answer, I hear "not yet." What is faith, after all, if we don't believe in second chances, and third chances, and.... We need to have the same kind of faith in our efforts toward change.

The story is told of Rabbi Akiva, one of the greatest of all Jewish sages, that he was an illiterate shepherd until past the age of 40. One day, sitting with his sheep by a stream, he noticed how a slow but steady drip of water had bored a hole clear through a mighty rock. Akiva thought, if that water can bore through rock, then surely Torah, which can cleanse more than water and slake thirsts that water cannot, can bore a hole through this thick skull of mine. And so he took up studies at that late age, and despite setback after setback, went on to become the wisest and most beloved sage.

We may not all have the patience of Akiva, yet we have each witnessed times when a struggle that seemed long past lost suddenly becomes surmountable. How are we going to keep working to stop climate change, despite the many inevitable setbacks along the way, if we don't think that a "no" from our board or elders or colleagues means only "not yet"? Rabbi Wolli Kaelter taught me this better than anyone when he was a rabbinic mentor at the Hebrew Union College. He took me to a board meeting, where he made a proposal that was defeated five to four. I asked him afterwards if he was disappointed. "Disappointed? No. Last year it was seven to two. In another year or two it will succeed." So, if your congregation has turned down spending on a windmill or an energy audit, if you can't convince your leadership to write letters to their Senators about climate change, or if your sale of CFLs only brought out four customers, do not despair. As the Talmud teaches in *Hagiga* (Sacrifices) 9b, reviewing a lesson 100 times cannot be compared to reviewing it 101 times. Maybe the next try will be the one to turn "no" into "yes" – but only if you believe that the last "no" really meant "not yet."

## You Are Not Alone

As noted above, Rabbi Tarfon's teaching is designed to help us realize that each of us is needed — and that we need each other's efforts as well. So we already understand that as we work with our human colleagues, we are part of a greater whole. But for people of faith, "you are not alone" goes one step further. Rabbi Nachman of Bratzlav, a Hasidic rebbe from the 1800s, wrote in his book, "Advice" (the chapter on Trust, number b1), that when people do something with faith, and in the course of doing so stumble, they should trust that the Holy One will help them get up again. We are doing our best to do God's work on earth. So doesn't it just make sense to let God help us in that work? Don't let your activism become separate from your faith; rather, make it one way that you express your faith, one way that your faith enriches and re-inspires you. For some, that might mean stopping every now and then to take a walk in the wonder of God's creation. For others, it might mean a quiet moment of meditation on how blessed this work is that we have been privileged to do. But we all stumble at some point, and — when we are honest with ourselves — we recognize that we often need help getting back up. So make sure you give yourself the time and space you need to feel how God is lifting you back onto your feet.

It will take an effort of many decades to turn around our global culture and redirect it into paths that are sustainable and just. The faith community has a unique voice and brings unique strengths to that effort, but that voice and those strengths will only make a lasting difference if we are able to sustain them year after year. For that to happen, we need to work in a consistent and committed fashion within our own congregations. I hope that the brief lessons above will make your efforts easier and more sustainable, and I look forward to us learning more lessons, together.

## 11

SR. PAULA GONZALEZ
SISTERS OF CHARITY
CINCINNATI, OHIO

# Love All Ways

"Regardless of how one understands the Eternal Creator, there
seems to be a widespread realization among different faiths
that we humans have forgotten that everything is interconnected,
that 'the Earth is the Lord's, and its fullness.'"

It is exciting to think that we live at one of the most transformative moments in human history. Over the past few years there
has been a growing chorus of voices across the planet, telling us
that much of humanity is ready to move out of its adolescent
phase into a more mature, responsible way of living. Documents
such as the Earth Charter (endorsed by over 2500 organizations
world-wide since 2000) and the UN Millennium Development
Goals (an international blueprint for a just and healthy world) are
inspiring statements of this growing realization that we're all in
this together. The opening words of the Earth Charter state the

unprecedented challenge facing humanity: "We stand at a critical moment in Earth's history, a time when humanity must choose its future. As the world becomes increasingly interdependent and fragile, the future at once holds great peril and great promise." Humanity's success or failure depends on whether or not we focus our attention and our efforts on *choosing* to create a future of promise, despite the enormous peril of our times.

But is this possible? Paul Hawken's recent book, *Blessed Unrest*, documents that there are over one million groups around the planet made up of "ordinary and not-so-ordinary people willing to confront despair, power, and incalculable odds in an attempt to restore some semblance of grace, justice and beauty to the world." The subtitle of this book suggests that a phenomenon such as this is unprecedented: *How the Largest Movement in the World Came into Being and Why No One Saw It Coming.*

## SEEKING THE PROMISE

In the past 35 years I have done about 1700 programs on global futures, ecological challenges, eco-spirituality and most recently, climate change. It has become increasingly apparent to me that if the faith communities were seriously engaged in these efforts, there could be major breakthroughs toward a sustainable future. What if we could all learn to collaborate – if we could be enriched by shared insights from our various faith traditions? The hunger for spirituality that is evident everywhere could be satisfied as people all over the planet become empowered to view their "environmental activities" as an integral part of a mature spirituality, and relevant to our challenging times. These could become "spiritual practices" instead, enabling us to "pray always," as scripture asks us to do. In every religious tradition there are mandates that urge respect and care for the created universe, of which humans are a part. Regardless of how one understands the Eternal Creator, there seems to be a widespread realization among different faiths that we humans have forgotten that everything is interconnected, that "the Earth is the Lord's, and its fullness." (I Corinthians 10:26) Our ecological crisis is evidence of our forgetting. Awakening to this realization may be the primary human agenda of the 21st century.

Back in 1980, when I was a college biology professor, I just decided one day to *do something* about the Earth instead of only talking about it. What might a Roman Catholic member of the Sisters of Charity of Cincinnati be able to do that would be a *visible* move in the direction of a sustainable future? I began at home, with our Motherhouse. Like many religious communities, ours was started on a farm; with the intention of ensuring our self-sufficiency, the Sisters moved to our 175 acres in 1869. Now, 140 years later, our buildings and grounds are in suburbia. The "visible" project I had in mind involved our large chicken barn. I asked for and got permission to convert part of it into a passive-solar, super-insulated apartment, where two of us have now lived since 1984. This was done completely by volunteers working on Saturdays for three years. Most of the building materials were reused, but we funded our purchase of new items (energy-efficient doors and windows, insulation, paint, etc.) through an alternative funding method based on nature's model of composting: we converted cast-offs into cash through what has since become my Giant Annual Yard Sale. As a result, our project was completed for $10 a square foot!

This was only a beginning, but an excellent testing ground for what's possible when we have a vision for the future. Ten years later I turned a large garage into a solar-assisted geothermal building called EarthConnection, a center for learning and reflection about "living lightly" on Earth. Since Cincinnati is quite cloudy in the winter, it is exciting to be able to heat this 4000-square-foot geothermal structure with last summer's sunshine. A 1.3 kilowatt photovoltaic system furnishes much of the current lighting load and will be enlarged to power the electric heat pump when more funds become available. And, to provide another example of the fact that solar really does work, this "solar nun" partnered with the Physical Chemistry lab students from our Sister of Charity College and solarized a golf cart. I will be ever grateful to my order for letting me give up teaching at our College to engage full-time in Earth ministry.

## OHIO INTERFAITH POWER AND LIGHT IS BORN

You could say that our original chicken barn was one of the birthplaces of Ohio Interfaith Power and Light (OhIPL). The story of OhIPL is about a collaboration that, I believe, is completely providential. For over a year I had been exploring the procedure for organizing a statewide group to promote sustainability in communities of faith. In the summer of 2007, I met Keith Mills, an elder in his Cleveland-area Presbyterian church, at the American Solar Energy Society meeting. I discovered that he too had been thinking along these lines. The synergy between us resulted in our first organizing meeting, in which 17 people from around the state came together and decided to take the necessary next steps. Clearly, Keith and I were not alone in our vision. Seven volunteered to be a steering team and committed to conducting an all-day meeting once a month. Early on, we recognized the importance of interfaith participation, which has since resulted in adding Jewish and Muslim members to our original all-Christian group. Soon, I hope we will have Buddhist and Baha'i representatives. The close community that has developed in this group provides an energizing and truly revitalizing experience for us all.

In the early days of organizing, we were fortunate to have Rev. Sally Bingham with us. Scheduled to preach in Cleveland, she generously agreed to come a day early — and so we dropped the routine meeting agenda we had planned, and instead OhIPL held its first "event." Over 100 people from around the state gathered for an informative and exciting program. We quickly generated enough interest that ten faith communities signed the covenant, becoming the very first OhIPL members. This was a real surprise, as we were concerned that we were not yet ready for an official launch of OhIPL. But they were certainly ready for us. We've moved our organizing efforts forward with renewed energy because of the success of our event, now very certain that the Spirit is with us!

## IPL in Action

The mission of the IPL movement is to increase energy conservation, energy efficiency and renewable energy, and to address seriously what may be the most important challenge in human history: global climate change. IPL is one of the growing number of initiatives underway today with the underlying goal of creating a sustainable world and caring for our common Home.

We want to do more than put a band-aid on the problems. In his excellent book, *Inspiring Progress: Religions' Contributions to Sustainable Development*, Gary T. Gardner of the Worldwatch Institute reminds us that "building sustainable societies is not simply about changing policies and technologies, important as these are. Sustainability requires a new understanding of our world and our place in it, a new appreciation of our relationship to nature and to a global community of human beings – a different worldview." I see this new worldview emerging. Thanks to our current communication technologies, the concept of reducing one's environmental footprint is becoming mainstream in a surprisingly short time. This provides an important challenge to IPL groups, both in our consciousness-raising activities and in advocating policy change at all levels – city, state, national and global. It is imperative that we keep the big picture in mind so that we do not become over-involved in a mere problem-solving approach, as many corporations and governments are doing today. "Greening" is becoming quite fashionable, but it is vital that this be true transformation, not just what you might call "greenwashing." Also, we must never forget that our faith-based approach is unique. And vitally necessary.

## RECOGNIZING THE SACRED

We can see changes happening now. It is clear that in contemplating our Earth, more and more people are beginning to realize that this truly is holy ground. Teilhard de Chardin, the Jesuit paleontologist, put it well: "For those who know how to see, nothing is profane – everything is sacred." We must develop a new way of seeing if we are to take on the enormous challenges facing us today. We 21st century humans have been gifted with new lenses through which to focus as we assess our global situation today.

If we ever feel alone in our journey, there are plenty of reminders that we are not. Imagine my delight when I received a DVD in the mail one day: *Renewal: Stories from America's Religious-Environmental Movement*. Billed as "a documentary about people of faith building a sustainable future," this powerful film gives brief descriptions of efforts being made by eight Christian, Buddhist, Jewish and Muslim groups to become caretakers of Earth. Interfaith Power and Light is featured as one of the examples. It is inspiring and encouraging to see how ordinary people are assuming leadership roles once they understand that the health of our Earth is seriously threatened by overconsumption and careless use of our planet's marvelous gifts.

In their book, *Coming Back to Life*, Joanna Macy and Molly Young Brown identify three dimensions of "The Great Turning," as they call it: activism that will stop the current destruction, the development of Earth-friendly alternatives, and a revolutionary shift in consciousness. "A sense of awe, gratitude, wonder, and devotion to our planet, life, and each other must arise from the heart."

Never before in human history have ordinary people experienced a "vision" such as the picture of our amazing planet from space. In 1969 we all shared the awesome view that has inspired so many to see the radical interconnection of all that exists here on Earth and beyond. In what I call "Revelation According to NASA," we can see the finiteness of our planetary home. Another insight that is emerging from the growing conversation between ecology and faith, or science and spirituality, is an increasing understanding of "Creation" as an emerging story in which each of us is a player. According to this new cosmology each of us is a part of what self-identified "geologian" Thomas Berry calls "the sacred Earth community."

The Earth Charter announces, "Humanity is part of a vast, evolving universe. Earth, our home, is alive with a unique community of life." This includes *all* the creatures, organisms and elements, and celebrates their radical interdependence. We humans are the only members of the community with the unique power of choice, and thus we have a huge responsibility for protection and care of "all our relations," as indigenous peoples think of their fellow creatures. The notion that we are invited to be co-creators of a new future unlike any past we've known is beginning to dawn all over the planet. What might happen if more and more people around the world saw the enormous opportunities for creativity and collaboration that our challenging times provide?

## A NEW REVERENCE FOR LIFE

Despite the great transformation I've seen over the last three decades of my work for the Earth, I still believe that not nearly enough people understand just how unsustainable we are today and thus do not fathom the scale of the changes that must be made. We are living through what may well be the third most important transition in human history. Our ancestors moved through the Tribal Era to the Age of Empire during which humans gained more and more control over nature. The last years of this period, the Industrial Revolution, have brought enormous changes in the relationship between humans and the rest of nature, and most of the challenges that we face today.

We stand now on the threshold of what might be called an Eco-Economic Revolution, a change on the same scale as the former major transitions. As we enter this period, we must come to grips with the social and ecological realities of our time. In *Our Ecological Footprint: Reducing Human Impact on the Earth*, Mathis Wackernagel and William E. Rees explain that around the late 1970s humanity began to live beyond the "ecoproductive capacity" of the planet. To provide the average US-Canadian lifestyle for all people would require at least three more Earths! Lifestyles in the industrialized world are possible only because billions of our human brothers and sisters across the planet live way below what is essential for a human life of dignity and hope. Thus, one of the most important contributions the many IPLs can make is to help people understand this truth, and the hard fact that a serious simplification of lifestyle cannot be avoided. Many of us feel trapped within our current consumer culture, not yet knowing that once we throw off these shackles, we will feel amazingly liberated. Of course, this is radical change we're talking about.

Obviously, conservation of all Earth's resources is essential. On our finite planet we humans are going to learn to live more simply, one way or another, either by choice or catastrophe. The Earth Charter reminds us that "The choice is ours: form a global partnership to care for Earth and one another or risk the destruction of ourselves and the diversity of life. Fundamental changes are needed in our values, institutions, and ways of living." We must creatively imagine, and then work toward, a sustainable society where humans and all the other creatures have a place at the table and live within the limits provided by nature's regenerative cycles. Rev. Sally Bingham, IPL's founder, though recognizing that religious environmentalism arrived later than it should have, makes it clear that its involvement is key in the search for a hopeful future. She has stated that "if the religious community is not involved in the sustainability movement, the transformation will not happen."

The reason for this seems clear to me. "Religious" or "spiritual" motivation may be the only way to engage large numbers of people around the globe in the transformation we need. For eons, indigenous people of many cultures have lived in intimate relationship with the natural world. Evidence of their lifestyles suggests that they acknowledged and responded to the divine (however they understood it) through an innate sense of the sacred. The divine spark within sensed the divine energy all around. Can we assume that this energy is available to the human community today? I do.

And how can it be awakened in humans everywhere to meet the magnitude of the task we face? My experience with groups during the last two years is that there is a growing hunger for something more meaningful than a consumer-driven lifestyle. Perhaps Interfaith Power and Light's example will *empower* and *illuminate* many more faith-based efforts. As our efforts multiply and we learn to re-connect with that divine spark, we humans may be able to make our own the closing words of the Earth Charter: "Let ours be a time remembered for the awakening of a new reverence for life, the firm resolve to achieve sustainability, the quickening of the struggle for justice and peace, and the joyful celebration of life."

## 12

LINDA RUTH CUTTS
ZEN BUDDHIST PRIEST
GREEN DRAGON ZEN TEMPLE
MARIN COUNTY, CALIFORNIA

# Call and Response:
## Resonance of Awakening to Global Warming (a Buddhist Perspective)

"Just as the Buddha called on the earth to bear witness to his right to be in peace on this earth, I feel now that the earth is touching us and asking us to bear witness."

H ow does Buddhism, a way of life and practice over 2,500 years old, respond to the crisis of global warming? As a Zen Buddhist priest, and one of the members of the Steering Committee of California Interfaith Power and Light, I am struck by both the shared concern for the earth that all the religions represented in this organization espouse, and the differences in image and language that are used to express that deep concern. I am deeply grateful for and inspired by Episcopal priest Sally Bingham's boundless energy and clear observing mind that have motivated such strongly committed people from all over the world to join her efforts to wake people up to the peril we all face.

I offer these thoughts about our shared love of place, traditional Buddhist attitudes towards nature, and the practices of universal compassion that help us to respond appropriately to our suffering world.

## HOME

I have the great good fortune to live on an organic farm in a valley that winds down to the Pacific Ocean. Living at Green Gulch Farm, Green Dragon Zen Temple, in Marin County, California, allows me to see a great variety of wildlife. During the spring and early summer we can sometimes glimpse fox families who have taken up residence under the different houses. They scamper across the roof of the meditation hall and relax in the sun or nestle in secluded spots to nurse their young. I marvel at the grandeur of the Great Blue Heron standing imperiously on the lawn, hunting gophers in complete concentration.

Then there are the owls. I personally have had numerous encounters with Great Horned Owls throughout the 15 years of my residence here. Once I met an unwavering individual who was standing in the roadway at 11:00 at night, when I arrived home. I got out of the car and we faced each other, gaze to gaze, in mutual amazement. After several minutes it spread its wide wings and flew straight up, in utter silence, into the tall Eucalyptus trees. Perhaps my most memorable chance meeting with the wild was during an early twilight walk in the hills above Green Gulch. I rounded a turn in the trail and beheld the awesome presence of a mountain lion! The tawny muscular body and long, thick tail stood still as we sized each other up – gaze to gaze once again – and then, also in a soundless moment, she slipped over the side of the hill and was gone. Unforgettable.

Equally wonderful to me is the organic garden and farm, rich with vegetables, herbs and flowers, the steaming compost heaps ready to nourish the soil, and the bee hives pollinating the crops in the foggy coastal air. All of this activity is tended and cared for by farm and garden apprentices, the residents and staff of Green Gulch, and enjoyed and admired by local folks and many visitors from all over the world. We are joined together in our appreciation of the beauty of nature and the dance of interconnected activity.

Reflecting on these everyday marvels of our world, a strong feeling of love comes up in me, not only for this particular place that I know so well, but for our whole earth and all of the beings – people, animals, plants, mountains, rivers and air – existing here together. This strong feeling for place, for home, is shared equally among all people, throughout all time.

And we now must accept, without a doubt, that the whole world, our home as we know it, is threatened. We need to respond, and our ability to respond – indeed our "responsibility" – is born from our awareness of our interconnection and our love and commitment to each other and our earth.

## AWAKENING

The word "Buddhism" comes from the root word *budh*, which means "awake." If one were to use an English word for this religion, one might call it "Awake-ism"; The Buddha is "the Awakened One." And the main teaching of Buddhism can be simply stated as "non-harming," if you will, or nonviolence; in Sanskrit it is "*ahimsa.*"

To what do we need to awaken so that we may live without causing suffering to ourselves, others and our environment? This simple teaching, non-harming, is not easily enacted and can really only be accomplished through loving-kindness and compassion born of wisdom. The actualization of wisdom in Buddhism is not knowledge that can be acquired, nor is it solely an intellectual activity, although these things are useful. Rather it is the thorough a realization of the interconnectedness and the impermanence of all beings. The deep understanding of non-harming — that we support and are supported by all beings, animate and inanimate, and that everything in the whole world is constantly changing in the web of cause and effect — can turn us in a new direction.

Once we awaken to our inextricable connection to the universe, and the knowledge that everyone and everything we care for is also a unique part of the universe, then a love for our world and for all beings flows forth from us. A strong wish for all beings to be cared for, to feel joy, and to be free from harm and suffering, naturally follows. Born of our connection and love, this desire must be expressed and enacted through body, speech and mind. The situation in the world calls out for a wise response, the core of which is compassion. One definition of the mind of a Buddha, of an Awakened One, is a mind of "love, concern, joy and generosity without measure." With a mind that functions in this way there is no end to the compassionate activity that can bring about the health and well-being of the earth.

## THE BUDDHA'S TEACHINGS

Shakyamuni Buddha, the founder of Buddhism, taught in India for about 40 years, and there is a vast literature of his teachings, as well as the teachings of others from the centuries that followed. Throughout his life he spoke about how to care for our environment through mindful action and how to live harmoniously by cultivating peace within our hearts. The life of the Buddha was characterized by a closeness with nature that we see in many stories: When he was born, his mother stood in a grove holding on to a tree. Later, at the time of his enlightenment, he realized his true nature of interconnectedness while sitting under a tree; and it is recounted that the Buddha died lying peacefully between two Sala trees whose flowers bloomed out of season in their expression of grief.

The night of the Buddha's Awakening he was sitting sheltered by the tree now called the Bodhi, *Ficus Religiosa*, or awakening tree, (the great-great-great-great-great-grand daughter of which is still alive in Bodh Gaya, India, and is thought to be the oldest historical tree). While he sat, with the resolve to remain there until he had understood the truth, all sorts of temptations and distractions assailed him. First there was the lure of greed for pleasure, next the trap of anger, and then the snare of self-criticism and undermining thoughts. Finally, the Buddha, asking for help, placed his right hand calmly on the earth. In this gesture, he called the earth to witness his right to be there, at this place, sitting under this tree of awakening. In this mythic evocation, the earth immediately responded to his call and, in the form of a woman, came forward and touched the Buddha's hand, meeting him and serving as the key witness to his claim to take his rightful place.

The Buddha's life of teaching was spent walking this earth, sleeping in forests, caves and parks, and giving talks to his followers on mountains and in groves. He taught his disciples, both monastic and lay, to live in harmony with the earth. The Buddhist Order had detailed proscriptions against killing living things, spoiling the earth or contaminating water. There is even a proper way to dispose of human waste. This attitude of deep respect for the beauty and diversity of the natural world, and the non-harming of our shared life was carefully passed down.

## BODHISATTVA

Caring for Mother Earth and the delicate natural balance that supports the source of life, and taking up an appropriate response to the peril we face now, is essential. One way to actualize this responsibility is through the practices of a Bodhisattva, or enlightenment being.

As Buddhism developed and spread out from India, it responded to the different cultures that it encountered, and so the teaching and practices also expanded. The ideal of a Bodhisattva – the embodiment of the vows to live for the benefit of all beings and not to abandon anyone or anything – characterizes a further evolution of the teaching as it spread throughout Asia, and more recently to the West. To actively take up these vows requires a response to the needs of the earth and all of the people who may suffer as the changes from global warming unfold.

The life of a bodhisattva is dedicated to the unending altruistic work of benefiting beings. One of the most well-known and beloved of the bodhisattvas is Avalokiteshvara, the Bodhisattva of Infinite Compassion. This bodhisattva is known by many names:

in China, Kuan Yin; in Japan, Kannon; in Tibet, Chenrisig. All of the names carry meanings such as "Sound Observer" or "The One Who Hears The Cries of the World"; each summons the image of one who listens carefully and responds accordingly. In some cultures represented as female, in other cultures, male, this bodhisattva is the personification of the compassionate energy that resides in each one of us. In many texts the bodhisattva shows us how to carry out the practice of being dedicated to helping others. This is not a passive model of compassion, but one that requires response and action.

In one text, The Flower Ornament Scripture (called the *Avatamsaka Sutra* in Sanskrit, composed in the 1st and 2nd century CE) the Bodhisattva of Infinite Compassion vows to help beings by carrying out the practice called "undertaking great compassion without delay." This is accomplished by dedicating oneself to protecting and guiding the sentient beings in our worlds, and finding ways to them in forms that they can understand. There are four skillful ways to guide people and to stay in harmony with them and ourselves as we address the inconceivable challenge of these times. We do this through generosity, kind speech, beneficial action and cooperation.

Avalokiteshvara continues:

*Perfecting this practice of unhesitating compassion, I have vowed to be a refuge for all sentient beings, to free them from fears of calamity, threat, confusion, bondage, attacks on their lives, insufficiency of means to support life, inability to make a living, the perils of life... miserable conditions, unknown hardships, servitude, separation from loved ones....physical violence, mental violence, sorrow and depression. I have undertaken to be a refuge for all beings from all these fears and perils. (from Book 39 of* The Avatamsaka Sutra, *translated by* Thomas Cleary)

This is the mind of immeasurable love and concern that cherishes all things, and even from 2,000 years ago addresses our current fears and the need for skillful action as we face this global crisis. This is the heart and mind of One Who Hears the Cries of the World. And these are practices not just for some specially developed person, but for each of us to manifest within ourselves. This is what is needed at this time. The perilous effects of global warming – the unprecedented loss of our diverse animal and plant life, the irreparable changes in crops and water sources, etc. – will be most devastating for the poor and for those who contribute least to the cause of these conditions. Unless we nurture our own hearts of infinite compassion, we will only create the conditions of great suffering for future generations.

Just as the Buddha called on the earth to bear witness to his right to be in peace on this earth, I feel now that the earth is touching us and asking us to bear witness. The earth, with her thin blue cloak of atmosphere, has a right to continue to live, to be happy and healthy. Right now the earth is calling. The voices of the atmosphere and earth and animals and water and mountains are calling. Can we hear the cries of the world? That call, if we are practicing "undertaking great compassion without delay," evokes a response. Call and response come up together. When there is a cry, there is hearing. This is spiritual communion, or resonance of awakening.

Do you hear it?

Our meditation and practices of morality will support us to hear it, to be fearless and calm and composed enough to hear it, and to act from our spiritual practice, to do whatever we can. Please join me and join each other and take up generosity, kind speech, beneficial action and cooperation, with the spirit of wisdom and compassion and love.

## 13

IMAM ACHMAT SALIE
MUSLIM UNITY CENTER
BLOOMFIELD HILLS, MI

# Anecdotes from an Eco-Jihadist

"We seem to instinctively know the power of a symbolic
act to clean our souls. Our beautiful souls will
create beauty all around us."

## MEMORIES OF CAPE TOWN

I was born on a farm in Cape Town, South Africa. Today, the farm
is part of a thriving city called Gatesville. My father, with his
horses and cart, rushed my mother to hospital. In my childhood
memories I am in the company of ducks and geese, hens, competi-
tion-quality cocks and horses, sheep, dogs and birds. Yes, we knew
for a fact that meat does not grow in the supermarket.

Cape Town is perhaps one of the most beautiful cities in the
world. With her unique flora (the proteas and fynbos, klip das-
sies and springboks) and fauna (the kwagga and wildebeast), and

the most beautiful beaches, Cape Town is like a loveable kitten or puppy; it is so easy to fall in love with them and overlook all their mischief. Our kitten, Mitten, entered our lives two years ago. Like a newborn, he wakes me up twice at night. My children shower him with love. I have to feed and care for him in other ways.

Cape Town has the same weather as San Diego and the beauty of San Francisco – it is ideal. As a student and later as a teacher I took many memorable hikes on Table Mountain and other mountains surrounding the valley. I recall the scenic drives along the beach from Sea Point to Houtbay that I took with my wife and children before we moved to Michigan. Sometimes, I extended the drive to return to Wynberg, where my in-laws lived. En route are a number of Muslim shrines, or *kramats*, where some of our Muslim pioneers are buried. For more than 150 years, Muslims at the Cape could not practice their faith in public. Today, Cape Townian Muslims honor those who practiced their faith in secret. And every year, pilgrims to Mecca pay their respects to these heroes who had to live their faith dangerously.

On these drives, you can see evidence of earlier sacrifices too: The Dutch colonists in the Malay Archipelago banished Malay and Indonesian scholars, princes, and other political exiles, to the Cape from as early as 1652. Some of these leaders, now buried in Oudekraal or Constantia, lived in the mountains or next to murmuring streams to practice their faith and to teach their religion in secret. They used the streams for their daily ablutions or ritual baths.

Our history is inseparable from the places I explored and the nature all around. I endeared myself to my mother- and father-in-law when I took them occasionally to these shrines where they could take ablution from the streams themselves, watch white cows at a farm adjacent to the Constatia kramat, or gaze at the Atlantic ocean at the Oudekraal kramat, and then recite some spiritual chants (*hajat* or *haddad*). My own parents loved their kramat visits to Lionshead, Makassar or Simonstown. Other kramats exist throughout the area. A kramat played a dramatic and vital role in Nelson Mandela's long period of incarceration on Robben Island. Mr. Mandela's friends and supporters would leave politically sensitive newspaper articles for him to find, discretely tucked under the colorful cloths of the Robben Island kramat.

When Muslims in Cape Town do their moon sightings for the commencement or the end of Ramadan, they do so in large numbers along the beach. They pray on the beach or even on the road at times. These moon sightings are opportunities to watch the sun set. I think of this ritual any time I watch the sun set over the water, wherever I am in the world. I cannot miss an opportunity to watch if I am close to a beach, and that crimson color as the sun goes down is still my favorite color. When we lived in Cape Town, every few weeks, my wife, the children and I would take our picnic basket out to the boulders at Sea Point, watch the sun set, and pray. Other weeks, we would go to Fishhook, where we'd see the penguins, or places where whale sightings have been reported, such as Hermanus and Camps Bay. On Houtbay beach, we would sometimes see a school of dolphins frolicking in the water. On off days or vacation times, I would study close to the beach where the sound of waves crashing against the wall would be my music backdrop.

## CREATING BEAUTY

In the midst of all this beauty, spills and other disasters at sea were particularly upsetting. Some of our best beaches were polluted with black oil and dead birds. Our family outings became less of a pleasure trip when we had to observe polluted beaches that took weeks to clean up. These beaches, in such sad condition, spoke to me of the way our civilization treats its earthly home.

Like inside, like outside, it seems to me. My own home gives me some insight into what needs to happen to stop such pollution. After my teenage sons have cleaned their room or done chores around the house, they get quite upset when their younger sisters litter. Success breeds success; cleanliness breeds cleanliness. Perhaps we should all visualize cleaning up our environmental mess, starting within our own thoughts, for inner purity helps us stay clean outside. I have experienced this in so many ways. For example, my community, the American Muslim Diversity Association, adopted a road recently. I never imagined the joy I could get from filling bags of trash. Here I was doing something, making a difference, creating a little beauty, and chatting with residents on the way. The occasional honk of appreciation made the sacrifice more than worthwhile.

We've often heard stories or seen images of the victim of a violent act jumping into a shower to scrub away the memory — as if the symbolic act of washing would remove the stain of the crime. We seem to instinctively know the power of a symbolic act to clean our souls.

Our beautiful souls will create beauty all around us. A beautiful architectural landscape, a decorated house, or well-designed apparel is all evidence of beautiful souls. As a child growing up in Cape Town I thought then that only Muslims were the most marvelous and beautiful people. Their homes, utensils, clothing and food dishes were very colorful. Their melodious voices, which they used for the daily call to prayer echoing through the city, were hauntingly beautiful. When I drove past their homes there as a child I would tell a friend, "That must be the home of a Muslim." Beauty and God were always intertwined, from my earliest thoughts.

The Prophet of Islam taught, "God is beautiful and loves beauty." To me, it follows that peace, too, is beautiful. Peaceful and compassionate people, with their inner beauty, cannot be racists, for they look at every person, regardless of his or her skin color, with admiration. I think of some of our great peace ambassadors of the 21st century — Mandela, Tutu, Kofi Anan, Oprah and Obama, among others — they are African and have inspired beauty in the human soul around the world.

Similarly, peace advocates are often environmentalists, and compassionate beings simply cannot be chauvinistic if they care about ants, penguins and endangered species. It goes without saying that a truly compassionate heart cares about the earth, as well as racial and gender justice. I remember so vividly when Africans in Apartheid South Africa complained about their white employers feeding their dogs prime steak portions, while they had to be content with crumbs and leftovers. Human beings definitely deserve our compassion as much as pets do; the heart that cannot understand this is sadly unable to see the beauty all around.

I am sorry to say that many green advocates become frustrated or even pugnacious when others just do not get it. They get stuck in too narrow a focus. It reminds me again of my teenage sons, who would speak assertively and harshly to their younger sisters who made a mess after a big spring cleanup. We forget sometimes that we are seeking a lasting and deep purity that is worth our persistence and patience.

## CREATING JOY AND PURPOSE

I have learned that there are times when it is best to endure disappointment with others, even with those we love, in order to come to a deeper understanding of our purpose in this life. In this regard, I must relate a personal story. My mom passed away "suddenly." She was diagnosed with breast cancer, but my five sisters decided to protect their three brothers, the weaker gender. I have since found other men too who were "spared" the agony of dealing with the impending death of a parent by caring women. The prophet of Islam said that women are made from an arch-shaped or bent rib (it must be no accident that the arc is the strongest structure in engineering). But little did these sisters realize how more painful and shocking the news of a "sudden death" is. Just before her death, my mother was on the phone for two hours with my sisters, saying her last words. On that day I was half a world away, delivering the inaugural sermon at the mosque in Sania, Canada. I did not know my mother was dying.

On my return, I received the news that she had passed onto the mercy of God. This was devastating. Two months later I would discover that my sisters knew all along that she had terminal cancer, and that her final prayer for me was that I'd be saint. Out of this most painful of experiences, I found a blessing. My mother knew me well; her prayer showed me just how well. She could see, as I now could, that my life's hope is to bring joy to the poor and dispossessed. My own experiences with nature, justice and beauty give my quest for joy its focus.

As a Muslim environmentalist, I find inspiration for my life and work from the primary sources of Islam: The Qur'an and the Prophet's example, the commentary on the Qur'an.

Now, allow me to share some important fundamentals about Islam for a moment. The Prophet to all Muslims is an exemplar. Does the Qur'an support all my deepest convictions and values? Certainly. The Qur'an and the Prophet's life and teachings both support the rights and freedoms we are familiar with. These rights include individual rights, gender and women's rights, human and civil rights, as well as eco- and bio-rights. The Qur'an and the Prophet condemned homicide, regicide, gendercide, genocide, eco-cide and biocide. We see this awareness of justice in the oldest history of Islam: The Prophet put an end to infanticide in 6th century Arabia. Early Muslims also ended the annual sacrifice of virgins to the River Nile.

A devout believer would care for his body by taking good care of it through regular exercise, a moderate diet, praying more than five times a day, fasting more than one month a year. The Prophet fasted almost half a year. Through fasting, we discipline our souls. Through fasting, a Muslim sides with the underprivi-leged. Through fasting, Muslims become advocates for people's rights, especially when they are voiceless and helpless. The Hajj, our blessed pilgrimage to Mecca, promotes non-racialism and gender equality — men and women wear white and use the same space to declare their presence before God. The Prophet was a peace advocate; in fact, Badhsah Khan and the great Gandhi took inspiration from the Prophet's nonviolent teachings and deeds.

The Prophet's faith made him fearless. So, by example, we see that the opposite of fear is not courage, it is faith. His confidence and conviction in God's assistance made him daring. But a hostile critique would remonstrate: "Don't you have a sword verse?" Read contextually, the sword verse encourages a defensive war against suppression of freedom of religion. And he or she might challenge, "Isn't there a very misogynistic verse in the Qur'an?" The Prophet never lifted his hand to any women. His life is the commentary of the Qur'an. Any Qur'anic verse must be understood through his life. At times, he allowed cultural practices to prevail, but demonstrated the ideal through his own practice. Faulty interpretations, not faulty teachings of Islam, are the culprit. The Prophet was a feminist, social justice activist, environmentalist, and a human rights activist. And what of Jihad? Is that not a violent thing? some might ask. The oft-misunderstood concept of Jihad really means the support of religious activism to improve the lives of others.

## CREATING IDENTITY

My faith in the Qur'an and the example of the Prophet form the basis of my identity as a Muslim environmentalist. I'm concerned about human and civil rights, creation and earth rights as well as planetary rights. Global warming, space junk and every form of pollution, are of equal concern to me. "Ethnic-cleansing," "group-areas acts," or any other euphemisms that conceal deep-seated hate and prejudice are dangerous to humanity. Discrimination often leads to elimination. Even democratically elected governments have committed genocide (We forget sometimes that Hitler was demo-cratically elected). Our mainstream media often neglect to look at the root causes of violence. Too often they study the symptoms of disease and not its roots. War is the terrorism of the rich and terrorism is the war of the poor. This statement may seem very sweeping but it does address the issue of state violence that gives rise to acts of terror. War has become a religion.

But despite these painful truths, Islam teaches that optimism is mandatory. In my own life, I have seen this to be so: The Clinton River a few miles away from our home in Rochester Hills, Michigan, used to be the most polluted river in the US. Today it is one of the cleanest rivers in the nation. We must be optimistic about the future, for the most polluted rivers, land masses, and even outer space, could become the purest and most useful of places. Nature has a resilience of its own that we can only barely fathom. It only requires that it have a willing and optimistic partner in humankind.

The Qur'an says that God has created everything for a reason: "Oh our Lord, You have not created this in vain" (3:176). A weed is often an herb with undiscovered medicinal value. And I've often wondered about cockroaches and mosquitoes too. What benefit, if any, does a cockroach serve? (My sense of wonder was very human-centered at times.) About 15 years ago, I attended a homoeopathic seminar. The lecturer told a story from India about a severe asthma case. The homeopath could not understand why his prescriptions did not work, so he went to visit the home of his patient. At the hollow bottom of the kettle he found a family of cockroaches. Instinctively, he knew that the cockroaches and the asthma were related. He used cockroaches in his homeopathic cure of asthma. The patient recovered "miraculously."

My college Biology lecturer, Mr. Scott, once commented on the value of mountain fires to the growth of new vegetation that could thrive only after the fire had destroyed the existing mountain flora. It's easy to forget the importance of fire to the cycles of nature when we only see its powers of destruction. I'd learned that when farmers decided to hunt down every wolf, the rat population multiplied and did great damage to the wheat crops. The wolves had kept the population in check. Wow, wolves help keep an ecological balance? There was more: "You know, when a pack of lions hunt, they do nature a favor by hunting the sick and weak ones," my teacher explained. This idea of symbiosis fascinated me. So many of nature's secrets were yet to be discovered. I learned to look at Nature with greater respect, in awe of the mysteries it holds.

The Qur'an claims that its own treasures cannot be exhausted. Scholars have observed that the Qur'an uses the same word, *ayah*, for a verse of the Qur'an (micro-revelation) and for any natural wonder (macro-revelation). If the treasures of the Qur'an cannot be exhausted, then neither can the wonders of nature be fully fathomed or grasped.

During my seminary days in the early 1980s, I founded a newsletter called *Altibyaan*. I wrote an article titled, "What on Earth are We Doing?" I was surprised and pleased that the Muslim scholar Muhammad Haroun, who became a good friend later, found it to be the only relevant article in the newsletter because it dealt with environmental issues from an Islamic perspective. For the last half century, Muslim scholars like Haroun, Nasser, Sardar, and many others, have expressed concern about the environment in their speeches and writings. I remember reading the Inquiry and Arabia magazines in which these scholars highlighted the causes and effects of environmental degradation. In 1998, I visited Mecca with five colleagues and 40 seventh-graders. There, a stone's throw away from the Kaba and the Sacred Mosque, we noticed how people would gather outside cafes in the street to watch *Animal Planet* or *National Geographic* documentaries. There are so many ways to give honor to God's creation. In Muskat, Oman, I observed how very passionate Sultan Qaboos is about the environment. He even instituted a fine for motorists who did not wash their cars. The avenues and beaches of Muskat were spotless and green. I felt proud to be a Muslim there. Oman is home to a minority sect of Islam, the Kharijites. The group started off as an extremist group but is today known for its pacifism. It is wonderful, and another reason for optimism, that a group that had a violent beginning now embraces non-violence or pacifism.

## CREATING FAMILY

In South Africa my mother had a tradition, passed on to her from her mother, of greeting the tiny ants and feeding them. She ordered us to spread sugar around the house to feed them. The same ants were often mean to us. When I migrated to Michigan, our tiny cottage had lots of wildlife, especially large carpenter ants and spiders the size of a quarter. My children were very young then, from one to seven. At times, they would scream or cry when they saw these giant ants or spiders. With repeated coaching they learned to greet these creatures without fear, and with respect. Today our daughters run up to dogs in the park to greet and play with them. They never tire of begging us to get a golden retriever or a pet monkey. Perhaps we'll relent one day.

Most nights, my children want me to read or tell them a story. The story would often be a story of a Prophet, saintly person, or life story, or anything with a moral lesson. They especially love the story of Solomon who spoke to animals, and the animals who served him. He used the courier services of the Hoopoe bird. Solomon is well known in our family; we named our daughter after Solomon's Queen, Bilqees.

My wife and I have experimented with everything natural: home birth, water birth, breastfeeding our four children until they were almost three, naturopathy and homeopathy, eco-halal (food that is permissible to eat under Islamic law, and also is produced in a sustainable manner) — as well as having our children together with us in the family bed for at least three years. We embraced a holistic view of life. We had a no-television policy for 10 years. To this day, our children use the television set to watch a weekly movie but no regular programs. We have grown accustomed to silence in our homes. The Qur'an, after all, was born after a protracted silence by the Prophet in a cave on the mountain. The most joyous sounds are the screaming of my children for joy or frustration at times with siblings. Perhaps the greatest torture to human beings would be to deprive them from the sight and laughter of children.

The natural and spiritual often coincide. My wife went into labor with our second son when we lived in a flat attached to a mosque. She hated hospitals. Her labor started at 10 A.M. on Monday, September 28, 1991. Our midwife advised her to tap into the energy of the mosque. Three hours later, at exactly one o'clock, the call to prayer was sounded. Our son's head emerged at the commencement of the call to prayer; his feet appeared as the call to prayer came to an end. As I have seen from my very early days in South Africa, the natural and the spiritual are often in alignment. And this is reason for joy.

## 14

THE REV. CHARLES MORRIS

PASTOR, ST. ELIZABETH CATHOLIC CHURCH

WYANDOTTE, MI

# Creation Care in a Carbon-Constrained World (a view from a Catholic parish priest)

"Generations of Catholic clergy have been formed in an image of the Divine relationship with humanity that ignores creation as the context for that relationship. In the great debate on the most important moral issue of our time, the voice of the Catholic pulpit has been somewhat muted."

ॐ

What a perfect spring day! Sunday, June 10, 2001, is auspicious not just because of the bright blue sky and the 70° temperature. At the St. Elizabeth rectory in Wyandotte, Michigan, where I live and work, we are celebrating. Dignitaries gather in the parking lot below while I, dressed in my black clerical suit and wearing a stole draped over my shoulders, carry a bucket of holy water to the roof on a ladder. For this day we are dedicating the installation of solar panels and a wind turbine. The Michigan Interfaith Climate and Energy Campaign has just gathered petitions from religious leaders across the State asking Congress to ratify the Kyoto treaty on the reduction of global climate emissions. A perfect day, indeed.

I think to myself: Today is Trinity Sunday. Last week was Pentecost. And how did the Spirit appear to the disciples in the upper room in Acts 2? It was in the form of a mighty wind (I picture our wind turbine) and tongues of fire (I imagine the sun's rays upon our solar panels). The prayer of blessing of the solar panels, written by Rabbi Fred Dobbs and Kim Winchell, a Lutheran studying for the Diaconate, has concluded. As I wend my way over to the wind turbine I take note that although it has been a beautiful day, the day has also been still — no wind. But at the exact instant the holy water touches the wind turbine, a gust of wind suddenly appears, the turbine spins and the assembled guests begin to gasp. I look up to heaven and give a thumbs-up sign.

That story serves as marker of a new *ruah*, the Hebrew word for breath of the Spirit. When the Divine Spirit blows over the waters of chaos in the opening account of Genesis (1:2), the process of creation begins and the conditions for life and for humanity are set in motion.

In this Eden world there is harmony between humanity and creation. Humans are put into the Garden to serve (*abad*) the Garden (2:15). Humanity's role is to be that of gardener, in a symbiotic, mutually fecund existence. Sin enters the picture when we humans forget that we are "a part of" and not "apart from" creation. The tempter, in enticing humans to eat of the fruit of the tree of the knowledge of good and evil, tells humans that they are independent of the Creator/creation and can be autonomous (3:5). With sin comes alienation. In stories such as the aftermath of the flood in Genesis 9, the first covenant God makes is not just with Noah and his family, but with "every living creature" (9:12). However, with the story of the tower of Babel (11:1-9), this attempt at usurpation of the Divine role in creation leads to alienation no longer just from creation. Now humans are separated and alienated one from another.

It is in that context that the prophetic voices, most poignantly that of Isaiah, call for reconciliation anew with creation. Isaiah envisions a world where "the wolf shall dwell with the lamb and the leopard shall lie down with the kid...the lion shall eat straw like the ox. The sucking child shall play over the hole of the asp, and the weaned child shall put his hand on the adder's den." (Is. 11:6a, 7b, 8)

And in case it isn't clear yet, the last book of the Christian Bible, the Book of Revelations, warns that God's wrath will destroy those who destroy the earth. (11:18)

The few illustrations cited above are, I believe, central to the story of God's intent for humanity to be partners in the enterprise of generative co-creation. Our task is to be gardener, not to cover the earth with asphalt. We were able to act under the illusion that we could asphalt the garden for the past few hundred years. However, as bleaching corals, shrinking glaciers and skyrocketing gas and food prices show us, we can no longer treat God's good earth as a dumping ground. We know now that is no more "away."

As Proverbs puts it, "Where there is no vision, the people perish." (29:18) It is role of the faith community (and I believe the artists as well) to awaken us both to the folly of our present enterprise and provide that vision of that new world, "a new heaven and a new earth." (Rev. 21:1)

## THEOLOGICAL TRAINING

In the case of my own tradition of Roman Catholicism, creation care is a natural outgrowth of our theological tradition. Catholicism has had an emphasis on the world as the Mystical Body of Christ and as sacramental. Consequently, a Catholic lens views the Divine as both transcendent and immanent. Both St. Augustine and St. Thomas Aquinas posit that these twin poles of revelation constitute the historical revelation as found in the sacred scriptures (the Book of Scripture and the Book of Creation) and in the Church's deposit of faith — and creation as revelatory of the Divine. As the Jesuit poet, Gerard Manley Hopkins wrote, "The world is charged with the grandeur of God."

All the more ironic then was that creation care was never mentioned as a moral call in any of my courses while I was in the seminary. As if through a radio telescope that picks up the echoes of the Big Bang, creation was treated as so much background noise. What makes this oversight even more unfathomable was that I had several courses in social ethics. I had a class in liberation theology. We had weekly colloquia where representatives from Physicians For Social Responsibility and Salvadoran human rights activists would challenge us on our response to justice in our ministry. We had an active social justice group, *Leaven*, and placement in a many social justice ministries. Yet despite all of the immersion I experienced in Catholic social teaching, the focus of justice was anthropocentric. Generations of Catholic clergy have been formed in an image of the Divine relationship with humanity that ignores creation as the context for that relationship. In the great debate on the most important moral issue of our time, the voice of the Catholic pulpit has been somewhat muted.

## RECENT CATHOLIC TEACHING

Recently, this stance has begun to change. The United States Conference of Catholic Bishops (USCCB), in their 2001 statement, *Global Climate Change: A Plea for Dialogue, Prudence and the Common Good*, says that "global climate change is about the future of God's creation and the one human family. It is about our human stewardship of God's creation and our responsibility to those generations who will succeed us. If we harm the atmosphere, we dishonor our Creator and the gift of creation."

The bishops apply three traditional elements of Catholic social teaching to their analysis. These were explained most succinctly by John L. Carr (Secretary of the Department of Social Development and World Peace for the USCCB) in his oral testimony in support of the letter before the US Senate on June 7, 2007:

*The Virtue of Prudence.* As Carr points out, it is simply right that we address a serious problem now rather than wait until it gets much worse to act.

*The Common Good.* Carr goes on to say, "The ethic of solidarity requires us to act to protect what we hold in common, not just our own interests."

*Priority for the Poor.* "The real 'inconvenient truth' is that those who contribute least to climate change suffer most from it."

The statement of the USCCB was powerful and pointed, as were similar statements from the world's religious bodies, but still there has been very little preaching from the pulpit on this great challenge of our time. Climate, coupled with peak oil (and in North America, gas), rising food prices, and loss of food as corn grown for fuel competes with corn grown for food, and the resultant turbulence felt throughout the world, are the key moral issues of our time. In Luke's Gospel, the lawyer asks of Jesus, "And who is my neighbor?" (10:29) This requires an answer that addresses all of my neighbors who may be affected for weal or woe by my actions. The poor who cannot adapt to impending climate chaos, the fish, birds, animals and other wildlife upon whom we depend for sustenance, and the future generations to be born, are all neighbors who have standing in the eyes of God. If the Church doesn't speak on their behalf, if people of faith who see the long view don't become a voice for the voiceless, then who will? Politicians? Media? Corporations?

Not only are we called to speak truth to power, but we as people of faith discover the integrity of this proclamation when we choose to "walk the talk," when we become the sermon we preach.

## PERSONAL CONVERSION

In my case, I experienced my own metanoia, or moment of conversion, in 1988, when I heard James Hansen, the noted NASA climatologist, warn Congress of the danger to our future that global warming poses. That same year, I read Thomas Berry's *Dream of the Earth*, and I was introduced to environmental justice by a parishioner of mine. Perhaps most profoundly, I attended a concert by the Paul Winter Consort, a group that interweaves the cries of humpback whales and wolves with world music and jazz. That concert struck a chord in my soul. From that moment on creation care would be at the heart of my ministry.

The following year I was assigned to an inner-city parish in Pontiac, Michigan. St. Vincent DePaul Church is a beautiful German Gothic structure. However, as with many urban and rural houses of worship, it is an old building, constructed in 1885, when coal was $3/ton. We had to celebrate daily Mass in a side room in the winter because we couldn't afford to heat the church above 40 degrees. Because it was so energy inefficient, we had very high utility bills. Further, like many similar parishes, we had great human need at our door and not a lot of resources coming in. I saw this as an opportunity to combine my own passion for energy/climate stewardship with sound fiscal management.

I had heard of an association, the Interfaith Coalition on Energy, a non-profit formed in 1980 among the Archdiocese of Philadelphia, the Board of Rabbis of Philadelphia, and the Metropolitan Council of Churches for Philadelphia. Their purpose was to help Philadelphia reduce energy waste through audits, bulk purchasing, workshops, a newsletter, etc. In 1992, I established contact with a staff member of the East Michigan Environmental Action Council, Kurt Martin. We thought our church could benefit greatly from the Philadelphia model.

Kurt knew of an energy expert in Toledo, Ohio, who would be willing to make the 21-hour trip to Pontiac to share his ideas about congregations banding together to leverage energy savings. In saving energy and money, I knew we would also be saving greenhouse gas emissions. We arranged an evening meeting in January of 1993 and I spread the word in our church. The evening came; the energy expert arrived. Kurt was there, and me...and no one else.

To say I was discouraged was quite an understatement. That was that, I thought.

When I transferred to St. Elizabeth Parish later that year I participated in eco-spirituality retreats under the auspices of an interfaith group in Michigan. In our own parish, we began an eco-justice group, Stewards of God's Creation, which still meets monthly to this day. Over the years we participated in civil actions, put on environmental fairs in the parish and participated in small faith-sharing groups on climate justice. (As I write this we are on the eve of showing the movie *The 11th Hour* to the community). The more I read and reflected, the more I became convinced that the great moral challenge of the age was the impact of our continued burning of fossil fuels on the world's climate systems. Related moral questions were: the vexing issue of population growth that increasingly taxes the earth's carrying capacity, the depletion of resources, the poisoning of the atmosphere and oceans, and the stresses on the world's water and food supplies. I was particularly concerned about the impact of pollutants on the poor and people of color.

During the 1990s, while serving as pastor of St. Elizabeth, I studied for and received a Master's degree in Urban Planning from Wayne State University, with particular reference to environmental justice issues. At the same time as I was completing the requirements for my degree, St. Elizabeth began its own journey to a smaller carbon footprint. We contracted with an engineering firm to conduct an energy audit of our facility. All kinds of opportunities emerged, from changing our lighting to a purchasing a new boiler. As we continued to make changes in our facility, we witnessed a drop in the peak energy demand of 60% over the course of five years.

By 2001 we had saved enough money to install a renewable energy system at the rectory. Although the return on investment for such a system was quite low compared to the return you could realize through implementing a simple energy-efficiency plan, I view renewable energy systems for houses of worship as a sacramental presence, a sign of grace and a method of public witness that a different world is possible.

At the same time, following my graduation in 1998, I had applied for and was accepted as a doctoral student in the Environmental Justice program at the School of Natural Resources and Environment at the University of Michigan. To attempt to study for a Ph.D. while working as a parish pastor at the same time proved to be an overwhelming challenge. I asked Cardinal Maida, my boss, for a sabbatical for a few years in order to complete the course requirements for the Ph.D. program. Instead, Cardinal Maida granted me a year's sabbatical to begin an Interfaith Power and Light program in Michigan.

## MICHIGAN INTERFAITH POWER AND LIGHT STORY

I had read a story about Rev. Sally Bingham's work with Episcopal Power and Light in the April 30, 2001 issue of Time Magazine. Her work bringing congregations in California together to obtain rebates for the purchase of renewable energy credits was very exciting. She was doing what I had tried to do years earlier in Pontiac. How excited I was when, after a story on St. Elizabeth's solar installation appeared on a public radio environmental news program *The Great Lakes Radio Consortium*, I heard from Rev. Bingham and a friendship ensued. Her guidance to us in Michigan was absolutely instrumental as we began the work of building a Michigan

Interfaith Power and Light coalition (MiIPL). As a result, we now have over 230 participating congregations, we've saved them over $2,000,000 in lifecycle energy costs and kept over 20,000 tons of $CO_2$ from ever entering the atmosphere.

We have also become a voice at the table in the promotion of energy legislation at the state level. MiIPL has been able to leverage our partnerships within the faith community to provide services from green vendors, such as lighting and Energy Star® appliances, at reduced rates for congregants and houses of worship. MiIPL has also provided workshops, put on an annual state conference and provided worship and educational resources to congregations as they seek to witness to creation care by reducing their carbon footprints.

## CONCLUSION

Our most powerful tool is to preach sermons that address creation and climate; promoting electricity fasts during Lent, for example, and energy efficient legislation are powerful witnesses to a world that can be. There are so many solutions to the problems that lie before us that we can initiate within our congregations: energy audits, lighting fundraisers, green shopping carts, and renewable energy seminars are good starting places. Utilizing the EPA Portfolio Management Benchmarking and the Cool Calculations calculator are yet more steps toward an eco-just world. A journey toward a sustainable faith community goes beyond direct electric use. It includes the reduction of hidden energy costs through the promotion of community organic gardens, composting and farmers' markets in the parish parking lot. It includes the reduction of water use through rain gardens, native planting and rain barrels

— all of which St. Elizabeth, my parish, is currently engaging in or about to create (in the case of the rain garden). It is for each community of faith, as they awaken to and reflect upon the enormous challenge of a carbon- and resource-constrained world, to decide.

Through models of shared wisdom, such as that practiced by Interfaith Power and Light, the Spirit of God can flow through the creative energy of the greater community of faith as we seek to usher in "a new heaven and a new earth."

## 15

THE REV. DR. GERALD L. DURLEY

SENIOR PASTOR

PROVIDENCE MISSIONARY BAPTIST CHURCH

ATLANTA, GA

# Let There Be Light

"Suddenly, I remembered the words, 'Let there be light,'
and the light of awareness flashed brilliantly in my
mind and began to bring my understanding of
environmental concerns out of the darkness."

ॐ

In the first four verses of the first book of the Bible and Torah, we read a very deliberate statement: "God created the heaven and earth." Since childhood, I have read and talked about the consequences of this powerful act, but it did not take on as much significance to me as when I became actively involved with actions regarding global warming, climate change and creation care. Genesis tells us that "God created the heaven and the earth." God realized that the earth was dark, so He created light from darkness and said that it was good. Light symbolizes the removal of ignorance, which can lurk in dark places undetected.

Most of my life I have considered myself as belonging to group I'll call "the enlightened masses." I did not necessarily consider myself an all-knowing person, but certainly one who attempted to keep abreast of current trends, and knowledgeable about issues important to those whom I am called to serve in my community. I was and am an individual who prides himself on his ability to read and understand the hard-to-grasp issues and the ones that others may only consider as transitory or of little significance to the well-being their community. I view talking with people, the media, conducting seminars or workshops, or utilizing any of the information-sharing platforms, as opportunities to learn and then disseminate data. I have discovered that those who may be "in the dark" about what is negatively impacting their lives are unaware of how they can effectively remove the shackles that have them bound.

## THE LIGHT DAWNS

At 18 years old, during my freshman year in college, I met The Rev. Dr. Martin Luther King, Jr. This was an early moment of illumination for me. It was near the beginning of the civil and human rights movement for justice and equality for all of God's children. Having grown up as an African American on the West Coast, I was not familiar with the stark, harsh realities of segregation and racism, which were being dramatically expressed throughout the South. I am certain now, as I look back over my life, that the vestiges of racism were indeed prevalent when I was growing up in the late '50s as they, at times, appear today. But I was virtually "in the dark" compared to African Americans living in other parts of America, because I was living in a multi-racial, multi-cultural world.

My first encounter with blatant discrimination was in Nashville, Tennessee, in 1960. It was then that I faced and felt the shackles of being black that were being placed around my hopes, my dreams and my aspirations. I had been recruited to play basketball at Tennessee State University. I had never ventured into the South, but the coach assured me that all would be well. This was also the year that the illustrious track team of TSU, staring Ralph Boston (who broke the long-standing record of Jessie Owens) and Wilma Rudolph (who won four gold medals), was the dream team at the Rome Olympics. I was excited about being in the presence of so many outstanding athletes, even though it was in the segregated South.

On one hot and sultry Saturday afternoon, I went into downtown Nashville to purchase a cap. I went to one of the leading department stores and tried one on that caught my eye. The saleslady, who was white, came up and told me that the hat would cost eight dollars and she would ring it up for me. Though I informed her that it was too small, she insisted I purchase it anyway. I asked to see the manager, who came and inquired about the situation. I quietly explained to him that the hat was too small and that I was not going to buy *that particular one.* He seemed to understand, but then turned to me and asked, "How do you know that hat is too small?" I replied, "I tried it on and it didn't fit." He looked at the gathering crowd, the saleslady, and finally very sternly back at me. Then he shouted, "N_ _ _ _ _, who would buy this hat after it has been on your wooly head?"

I was stunned and scared as they took the money out of my pocket and threw me, and the hat, out on the sidewalk. Little did I know then that this incident would prime my emotional, civil and human rights internal pump. From then on, I joined picket lines, mass rallies and marches, and I gave speeches to end segregation and discrimination based on race and color. The light of justice was lit and my purpose for living was no longer in the dark.

I have dedicated most of my adult life to attempting to say, as Moses wrote in those first few verses of Genesis, "And the earth was without form and void, and darkness was upon the face of the deep. And God said, 'Let there be light' and there was light. And He saw that the light was good." God, from the beginning of time, knew that His creatures had to be enlightened if they were to protect and care for His earth.

## THE LIGHT SHINES DOWN

When one is in darkness, he or she is blinded to the truths and realities that exist all around. One can assume or be made to feel that something is not right, but it is not clear exactly what is wrong or why conditions and circumstances that seem ever present don't quite make sense. When you are in darkness, you just don't know or understand what is transpiring in and around your well-being or in the world in which God placed you.

As I committed my energies to making the world a better place for all of God's creatures, I, because of ignorance and being in the dark, was neither familiar with nor concerned about the destruction of the environment in which God had placed His people. However, I was deeply, sincerely and compassionately concerned about racial justice, civil and human rights, and being dedicated to assisting people understand that God created us all equal. My goal was to bring light into some very dark corners of our society. I was personally unaware and not particularly concerned about the physical and environmental world in which we lived. As I reflect over the last three years, I can honestly say that on environmental issues I was totally in the dark. I was content, in my world, and satisfied that those who had other callings would sufficiently pursue the goals they felt were important. Our paths would possibly never cross.

Then in 2006, I was invited by Mrs. Laura Sydell, the founder of animated series *Captain Planet* and the daughter of Ted Turner, to see a movie called *The Great Warming*. I reluctantly accepted the invitation. Being in the dark on this topic, the movie held very little interest to me. But because Laura was a friend, I went. Initially, I sat there not believing that I was in the midst of a group of who had little else to do with their time and resources than to talk about the extinction of polar bears, climate change, global warming, carbon dioxide buildup, greenhouse gases, wind energy, solar power, biomass alternatives, fossil-burning fuels, melting glaciers, massive digging of coal mines, deforestations and blah, blah, blah. What did all of that scientific mind-gaming have to do with the lives of everyday people? — and especially the African American community, where we were confronting social injustice, racism, political disempowerment, unequal education, inequitable health-care opportunities, disproportionate unemployment and high crime rates, to cite just a few really serious human concerns.

Initially, I felt put upon to have to sit through what seemed to me like an indoctrination film/seminar. I felt that it had been produced as a kind of Message of Mass Distraction to deter people like me from the more serious issues that were destroying human kind. Then about half way through the movie I began to see, feel and understand something that was so real and truly was destroying all human, plant and animal life, equally. Suddenly, I remembered the words, "Let there be light," and the light of awareness flashed brilliantly in my mind and began to bring my understanding of environmental concerns out of the darkness. The truth about the condition of the environment and what we are and are not doing was absolutely blinding. I tried to cover and protect myself from it, but the light came in anyway and removed the ignorance in which I had so comfortably lived. When you are enlightened, you must then make choices about whether you will remain in the darkness of ignorance or seek the light of understanding.

I now realize and understand that we must work together, across religious and scientific disciplines, to create, inform and nurture a more environmentally sensitive government and citizenry. I have become a staunch advocate who will assist in creating a grassroots movement throughout and within my areas of influence, which includes African American pastors, the African American community, the national religious environment, and people in many other parts of the world.

Together we must work diligently to pass legislation that will reduce global GHG emissions and fossil-fuel consumption throughout the world. I accept and believe the alarming facts that 40% of US waters are too polluted for fishing and swimming, 100 million Americans are breathing unhealthy air, and one-sixth of all women of childbearing age carry enough mercury in their bodies to negatively affect the brain of a fetus. It is not enough to have political and social rhetoric about global warming. We are facing the consequences of years of frivolous negligence, and nature has responded in ways that we can neither control nor alter immediately for our own convenience. We must make a comprehensive evaluation of the existing situation and take aggressive action to do whatever we can, as best we can, while we still can, to balance the current realities of nature and our own past, reckless abandon. We must do it now, because time is running out.

The light is on and it must continue to shine in all of our lives, to let us see that most living things are being harmed because we are not aware nor globally concerned about what it will take to save the environment. Myanmar was devastated by a cyclone, China was rocked by an earthquake, Darfur has little water, and island populations are having to migrate to other lands and countries to survive. Here in America we are experiencing a disproportionate number of hurricanes and tornadoes, which have created frequent flooding of historic proportion. God said, "Let there be light" and He separated the light from the dark and He said the light was good. It is good for us to be in the light, which has shown us our shortfalls. The question now is whether we close our eyes and minds once they have opened to the light and our responsibility to act immediately on these issues.

The time has come for civil and human rights activists, clergy, scientists, businesspeople, environmentalists, climatologists, politicians, legislators, old and young people of all colors and nationalities and any person walking in the light, to join forces creatively to stop, or at least slow down, global warming. When people "of the light" walk "in the light" there will be a mass movement leading yet more people from the dark, greedy, self-serving destructive environmental patterns of behavior that have kept us separated and divided on this question of climate change. None of us can be very effective in our different and varied personal areas of concern if we are destroyed by the ravages of a toxic environment. The environment surrounds and engulfs all of us regardless of the movement to which we are committed.

We can no longer afford to remain isolated in our individual spheres of influence. When we do not coordinate our efforts, we collectively squander the bountiful resources that God has provided and allowed us to use for millennia. Now that the light has entered these once-dark areas, we must enlighten those who remain in the dark. It is imperative that we recognize the gravity of the current condition, and then make ourselves as knowledgeable as possible about what can be done to maximize our collective efforts. Today, I encourage you to become a committee of one, asking and seeking out people and/or places where your specific skills can be utilized to enhance the environmental movement. The time has long since passed where we can feel comfortable in our own little "unlighted worlds." Those who are no longer in darkness must use their enlightened consciousness to save God's creation. We must, more than ever, reflect on the words of the Creator when He said, "Let there be light and it was good."

## 16

THE REV. FLETCHER HARPER

EPISCOPAL PRIEST, EXECUTIVE DIRECTOR OF GREENFAITH

NEW BRUNSWICK, NJ

# I Believe Three Things

"Loving wilderness and open space is important, but it is
not enough. We must learn to love creation in its broken places –
in places we have broken. Seeing these places and learning
their stories can be a first step."

❧

I believe three things about the relationship between religion and
the environment. These beliefs shape my life as a religious-environmental leader and as the executive director of GreenFaith, an
interfaith environmental coalition. I see their related dynamics play
out in my organization's work every day.

## WHAT ARE THESE BELIEFS?

First, I believe that people's most powerful experiences of God
almost always happen outdoors. Pastorally, most religious leaders

don't know what to do with these experiences — whether to reject them as "worship of creation" or to approach them hesitantly, uncertainly. I believe religion must embrace them to be a force for ecological good.

Second, I believe that capitalism as currently practiced tends in an addictive direction and shapes individuals to believe that consumption is life's purpose. Until this style of capitalism changes, creation is at risk and people will be stuck in consumerist bondage until they realize that spiritual freedom and moral decency come, in part, through responsible consumption.

Third, I believe that oppressed communities around the world suffer disproportionately from environmental degradation, their health threatened and their access to power over their own environment denied. I believe that religious-environmentalism must include political activism to create safe, healthy environments for communities of color and poor communities, and seek greater power for these communities to protect their own environmental health.

All religious-environmental work is connected to these themes. In this essay I would like to share several stories about ways that GreenFaith has engaged them.

## SPIRITUAL EXPERIENCE AND THE ENVIRONMENT

Several years ago, an African American Baptist pastor told me the following story:

*I grew up in south central LA. I was Baptist, and I must have sung "How Great Thou Art" a thousand times by the time I was 12. Then, one summer, my Boy Scout troop organized a trip to climb Mt.*

*Whitney. It was a very difficult, challenging climb. I had never had to work so hard physically as I did to get to the top of that mountain. But when I did, and when I looked around at the hundreds of smaller peaks that fanned out below where we were standing, when I looked at the huge expanse of land that I could see — then, for the first time, I could say "How Great Thou Art" and mean it.*

Since 2002, I've spoken with hundreds of adults about their spiritual experiences in nature — all unique, but each containing a strong connection to the sacred. Invariably, it is a captivating thing to do.

Over and over, in different settings, the same pattern of events unfolds. Individuals gather. They are invited to sit in silence and to recall a spiritual experience, a deeply meaningful experience they've had in nature, in the environment. I don't define the terms beyond this. It's not necessary.

After a minute, no more than two, I ask people to share their stories. There is little delay. One person describes an experience, then another, and another. People of all ages take part, not just those accustomed to talking in small group discussions. People of all ages speak, men as often as women. As the stories emerge, everyone in the room becomes more animated. Those telling the stories speak slowly; they choose their words carefully and artfully, modulate their voice tone and pace of speaking, and express what I see as a re-ignited life. Their facial muscles shed the customary tightness of involuntary stress, and their expressions become more complex, nuanced. Everyone becomes quiet. For almost every-one who takes part in this exercise, it is the first time they have ever spoken about these experiences, frequently among the most powerful spiritual experiences they have ever known.

The story above is about awe, one of the common themes in people's nature experiences. Here is a second kind of story:

*One summer when I was in my early 20s, I was doing a cross-coun-try trip to the southwest. My friend and I were driving in New Mexico or Arizona and got lost on a side road. We just settled in and decided to sleep in the car or just outside. We parked and were sitting outside the car when the sun went down. It was spectacular with the colors. My friend went to read; there was a summer lightning storm on the horizon 50 miles away. It was completely soundless, and the lightning illuminated the desert. I watched it literally for hours.*

This was told to me by a forest expert from a US environ-mental regulatory agency. His experience is one of many I have heard in which an individual comes face to face with an intense, captivating, unforgettable beauty, a beauty which can, at a distance of years, remain remarkably fresh and serve as an entryway into deeper regions of the soul. In stories about awe, what matters most are the size and the power of the scene and, by extension, its Architect. In stories about beauty, what matters most is the artistry of the scene, not its size. The focus here is on skill, not might – a different face of God.

These first two types of experience are relatively easy for peo-ple to share with one another. The same cannot be said of the third kind of story.

*Sitting on our small deck, knitting and resting old legs, I am entertained by my spiritual sister, an equally old pine tree. She is very tall, prob-ably 40 feet or so, and is at least as old as I am. She leans a bit; so do I. In her care are many birds that I watch with pleasure. They love and fight and nest in the tree. At Christmas time, pairs of cardinals decorate her limbs.*

*She is still green, covering lots of old brown branches, like my gray hair covering the black. We both soak in the sun and the air and are trying our best to live lightly in our worlds. One day in the not-too-distant future she will fall and fertilize the earth, as I will do. It's a consoling thought. We have children and grandchildren that give us the continuation of life. A bit of the divine in the tree and me. Yes, that's close to what I believe.*

*When my mother died, I was pregnant and needed her. I went to the church to be quiet and cry. The church was locked and the priest was standing outside. He knew me but did not unlock the church. I don't know why, but it was a nail in the coffin of my traditional beliefs. We had nine family-related deaths in one year. I learned to watch the red setting sun and was calmed, soothed and grateful, at least for a moment. I began to like digging in the dirt instead of cursing each weed. I started to spend Sunday morning in the woods. Was I losing long-held beliefs or simply changing them?*

*There is a bit of the divine in the trees and the creatures who reside there.... I believe my tree and all other living things believe and feel in their particular living ways. I want to work on being as good a human as I am able, just as my tree does her job with grace and elegant treeness.* ("Living Life with Elegant Treeness," by Ruth Kamps, on *National Public Radio,* Morning Edition, *August 15, 2005*)

This story exemplifies the third kind of experience, which I call "expanded communion." These stories are more complex than the first two kinds, in which the natural world remains as an object. They respect nature as a source of inspiration and admiration, while keeping nature as an object, an "it." And while these two stories may approach the boundary of claiming that nature has a spiritual dimension, they don't explicitly cross it. By respecting that boundary, or by not discussing it, they remain relatively safe.

That can't be said of this third kind of story. It declares, very clearly, that a tree is a being in a manner far more "human" than we normally recognize. Or more. Ms. Kamps asserts that there is "a bit of the divine in the tree and in me." This is the heart of the matter. Today, only in two arenas — pets and gardens — does our culture allow us to speak about some other subjective presence existing in the world in addition to human beings. Outside of those two areas, people who speak about trees or animals with personalities, or who see God inside them (not just through them), are called "tree huggers." Their perspective is put down.

I don't believe that our society will achieve ecological sustainability if we have not known the joy of nature's beauty, been silent in the face of her wonder, felt grateful when we've been reconnected to the wider community of creation. We need to rebuild our basic bonds with the earth, so that we can hear the call to sustain that which sustains us.

## CONSUMPTION, RELIGION AND THE EARTH

Gary Gardner is director of research at the Worldwatch Institute, a leading environmental and development think-tank in Washington, DC, publisher of the annual State of the World report on the condition of the global environment. Gary told me this story in 2004:

*Recently, I had a good friend visit me from out of town. He eats cereal for breakfast in the morning, which I do not, so before he arrived I went out to the grocery store to buy him a box of cereal.*

*I walked into the supermarket aisle where the cereals are displayed. I was stunned when I was faced with the huge array of breakfast cereals. Out of curiosity I began to count. There were over 120 different brands, all on display in that one aisle.*

*This made me think. In my work, which focuses in part on Third World and development and the environment, one of the operating assumptions economists make is that a country becomes more developed when its citizens have more choices. This is obviously true in a number of important ways, but when I stood in that supermarket looking at the shelves of different breakfast cereals, I began to see that there were real limits to the truth of this understanding of linking development, choice and consumption.*

*Then, I began to think about some of the most important choices I've made in my own life, choices about my job, my marriage, my family. When I chose my job, I didn't have 120 options — I had only a couple, and choosing from between this small number forced me to become clear about who I was and what kind of work I valued most. When I was choosing who to marry, I didn't have 120 options — I had one person that I chose, and committing to that single choice, over the years, has shaped me in deeply important ways. These experiences of limited choice have been some of the most important occasions for spiritual growth in my entire life. I wouldn't be the person I am today if I hadn't wrestled with these choices.*

This story has both religious and environmental implications. In addressing one of our culture's shortcomings — a consuming commercialism — it invites us to recognize another reason that religion is related to the environment. Both religious and environmental leaders believe that human individuals and cultures find well-being and a truly good life, not through the obsessive pursuit of material consumption, but rather through reverence offered to a greater power and through service offered to a wider community. The time has come for religious and environmental leaders to find common language and to develop shared strategies to make it clear that human restraint in relation to the earth is necessary for human survival, flourishing and genuine happiness.

Often, GreenFaith encourages religious education classes to take the Ecological Footprint Quiz, a 15-question survey of personal consumption habits focused on transportation, food and housing. I've come to think of the act of administering this quiz as a form of ecological confession. Most people live with a vague sense of the recklessness of US consumption habits. When they see that if all humanity used resources at their current rate, it would take five or six earths to provide the raw materials we'd need, they are usually sheepish or ashamed. "You just knew it wasn't going to turn out well," said one woman after taking the quiz. "It was embarrassing, frankly," said a pastor. Our purpose in using the Footprint Quiz is not to inflict guilt gratuitously. But the Quiz, and other tools like it, have an important place in raising moral-ecological awareness. As a pastor, I don't see anything wrong with people wrestling with the areas of their lives where improvement is needed. Too often, our culture peddles the false hope that consumption will save us. Our religious traditions know better. "Man does not live by bread alone," said Jesus to the devil (Matthew 4:4). This verse has a challenging relevance for our society.

On probing deeper, there is hope. Many people feel hoodwinked by the marketing onslaught. Many realize that they are not more fulfilled by more stuff. Many people want to change. But it is countercultural in America to seek to consume less, to reduce the amount of resources one uses. Most people who start down this path feel some anxiety at their separation from the predominant cultural norm. I have found repeatedly that people benefit from support, from a sense of community, when they encounter these feelings. Religious institutions can offer this support. Teaching mindfulness about consumption, and offering support for reducing our ecological footprint, should become a new norm in religious institutions, a fundamental dimension of what it means to be spiritually mature.

## ENVIRONMENTAL RACISM, ENVIRONMENTAL JUSTICE

My friend and colleague Ana Baptista, an environmental justice activist and scholar, received her Ph.D. from Rutgers University in New Jersey. She grew up in Newark's Ironbound section, a predominantly immigrant, working-class neighborhood that suffers from a range of environmental health threats.

*Growing up in the Ironbound neighborhood in Newark, I experienced firsthand the impacts of environmental injustice. Although I felt a great sense of pride for my hardworking, diverse community, I could never shake a sense of resentment about the degraded conditions we lived in — the abandoned dump sites, foul odors, lack of green space. When we'd take school trips to the suburbs, I was shocked at how pristine everything looked and thought to myself, Are my classmates and I not worthy of this as well?*

*At the time I didn't know these issues were central to environmental justice; I just wanted to be part of something that could improve conditions in my community. I was heavily involved in the leadership of my local Catholic Youth group. The environment was some foreign hippy issue to us, but in the context of social justice, service and compassion, I found I could rally my friends into action through clean-ups and other local activities. As a teenager I joined my first protests of hazardous waste incinerators and I haven't stopped since. I started my academic career dedicated to traditional studies in ecology, which later evolved into an interest in public policy and urban studies. The problems I experienced in Ironbound, I realized, were not just the product of isolated issues in our community or mere physical problems related to local industries, but were the result of economic, social and political problems facing communities like Ironbound throughout the world.*

*My journey has brought me full circle. I have completed my doctorate at Rutgers University's School of Planning and Policy, focused on environmental justice policy development and working part time as an environmental justice coordinator for the same organization that first invited me to join the incinerator protests as a teenager, Ironbound Community Corp. I still try to channel those youthful feelings of anger into activism based on compassion for members of my community and a deep sense of justice.*

Twice each year, GreenFaith organizes a tour to introduce religious leaders to issues of urban environmental health and justice. We visit contaminated sites, inviting local environmental activists to describe their struggles. A recent tour took place in February 2008, when 140 people gathered at First Hopewell Baptist Church in Newark. There were African American clergy, lay leaders and synagogue members. Adults from a large Catholic Church joined a youth group from a suburban Episcopal parish, students from Princeton University, Drew Theological School, Bergen County Community College and Islamic schools from Paterson. It was a mixed group. People drank coffee and ate doughnuts in the church hall before walking through the bright, crisp day to board their bus.

Over the next three hours, they were introduced to a dizzying array of contaminated sites and to the issue of environmental justice. It has been well proven that communities of color and low-income communities suffer the worst effects of environmental degradation. Our tours are an introduction to that reality. We visited the Pabst Brewery, on Newark's western border. The facility is massive, half demolished, with three derricks dwarfed by the remaining building shell. While developers and politicians have sought to dismantle the brewery and rebuild at a profit, the community has been exposed to extensive amounts of lead-paint dust and tons of airborne asbestos. These toxins have been pulverized and spread around the community. Local leaders such as Paradise Baptist Church's Pastor Jethro James have fought, with some success, to protect the community's health.

The next several stops were in Newark's Ironbound section, a vibrant community described in Ana Baptista's story above. The array of contaminated sites is stunning. Athletic Field B was built in 1999 to provide much-needed recreation space for the community. In 2007, the state ordered the field closed because the artificial turf had deteriorated and released dangerous amounts of lead, endangering thousands of children. A nearby facility, abandoned in the 1990s, contains high levels of PCBs and other toxins. The EPA recently agreed to remove some of the site's most toxic soil so that the site could be considered as the location of a future school.

One of our final stops was at the Ironbound incinerator, the state's largest garbage incinerator. Located within a half mile of two low-income housing projects, it's one of New Jersey's largest legal emitters of mercury, a potent neurotoxin. GreenFaith and the Ironbound Community Corporation have entered into negotiations with the incinerator's owner, seeking to reduce these emissions. Less than a mile away is the Diamond Alkali Superfund site, one of the most toxic concentrations of dioxin in the world. Much of the Agent Orange used in Vietnam was manufactured here. Now, the poisonous remains sit underneath a concrete mound on the banks of the Passaic River.

Almost everyone experiences these tours as an introduction to an alien reality. Yet this dimension of reality is something with which religious institutions must grapple if we are to become leaders in restoring creation. Loving wilderness and open space is important, but it is not enough. We must learn to love creation in its broken places, in places we have broken. Seeing these places and learning their stories can be a first step.

In our experience, it is not easy for religious institutions to address these issues. For predominantly caucasian congregations, environmental racism is a painfully shameful reminder of the scope and destructive power of racism. For communities of color, environmental injustice often seems like just one more item on a long list of oppressions from which they already suffer. But religious-environmental work without an engagement of environmental justice is inadequate. At GreenFaith, we hear a clear call to work for a safe, healthy environment. For all people.

## CONCLUSION

Protecting the environment is finally coming to be recognized as one of the great moral issues facing humanity. More and more religious groups are getting involved. I've argued in this essay that religious groups should engage these issues from three different vantage points: spirituality, stewardship, and justice. I've shared stories showing how GreenFaith has done this work. It is encouraging to see so many other religious leaders beginning to respond to this call.

One final note: It is common, and tempting, to think that the religious-environmental movement just represents our efforts to protect creation. This is true. But there is a second dimension that is as, or more, important. Engaging this issue is vital to a strong future for religious institutions. If religion cannot provide meaningful leadership on one of the most pressing issues facing the human family, then it will lose its ability to present itself as a moral force. It will lose relevance and credibility. And, rightly, it will lose influence.

The environmental crisis cries out for a widespread, strong religious response. The environment *needs* religious leadership. But the reverse is true as well. For the sake of the earth and of religion, this is an opportunity that religious leaders cannot afford to overlook.

## 17

LAUREL KEARNS
DREW THEOLOGICAL SCHOOL
WITH BETH NORCROSS
GREEN SEMINARY INITIATIVE

# Greening Our Seminaries

"This task will take theological education to new places,
to widen even further its domain"

❧

In 2007, six major figures in eco-theology spoke before a standing-room-only crowd in San Diego, California, and gave a rallying cry for theological schools to take seriously their obligation to prepare religious leaders to meet the looming ecological crisis. John Cobb, Cal Dewitt, Norman Habel, Sallie McFague, Larry Rasmussen and Rosemary Ruether challenged seminaries, theological schools and schools of divinity to infuse theological education with an earth ethic and to create physical and spiritual communities to support that ethic. In response to this challenge, the Green Seminary Initiative was launched. Its mission is to equip pastors, rabbis and other religious leaders with the theological perspective and the tools needed to lead their congregations and communities in responding faithfully to the ecological and socioeconomic challenges ahead, for they are intertwined. In support of this goal, the Initiative encourages institutions to model eco-justice and ecological care in their curriculum, community life, buildings and grounds, and institutional practices. This is an urgent task. As Ruether commented at that American Academy of Religion forum in San Diego, our current way of life is destroying our planet and us:

> *It is thus critical that our entire culture and way of life transform itself to cope with this challenge. Changing our spirituality and worldview is a crucial part of this transformation. But most of us find that challenge too difficult and foreign to our entire socialization to know what to do. Thus we court disaster by being unable to pay attention to what is happening. We wait for the levees to break and the water to begin to rise in our living rooms before fleeing pell-mell for higher ground. But we cannot give up. We need to continue to press this issue throughout our society, but particularly, for theological educators, in theological education. Eventually we will be heard, even as the time grows later and the urgency increases.*

## HISTORY OF THE MOVEMENT

Long before the news media, or for that matter, many of the rest of us, started paying attention to religion's response to global climate change, religious voices were issuing a call to address the ecological crisis. In a June 1939 radio broadcast from Jerusalem, Walter Lowdermilk proposed a poignant and prescient 11th Commandment:

*Thou shalt inherit the holy earth as a faithful steward, conserving its resources and productivity from generation to generation. Thou shalt safeguard thy fields from soil erosion, thy living waters from drying up, thy forests from desolation, and protect the hills from overgrazing by thy herds, that thy descendents may have abundance forever. If any shall fail in this stewardship of the land, thy fruitful fields shall become sterile stony ground and wasting gullies, and thy descendants shall decrease and live in poverty or perish from off the face of the earth.*

In 1964, Joseph Sittler showed the connection between faith and the environment in *The Care of the Earth*; in 1970, evangelical Frances Schaefer wrote *Pollution and the Death of Man* (and included Lynn White's treatise on "The Historical Roots of the Ecologic Crisis," which had first appeared in 1967); and in 1972, theologian John Cobb asked *Is it Too Late?* — and set out his case for ecology theology. In the US, several denominational statements were issued in the 1970s, and denominational offices and staff dedicated to the issue appeared in the 1980s, as did internationally known "centers of practice" such as the evangelical Au Sable Institute, under Cal DeWitt, and the Genesis Farm, under Sister Miriam McGillis.

The World Council of Churches held various conferences leading up to the Justice, Peace and Integrity of Creation theme proposed at the 1983 Canberra meetings, and in 1986, leaders of world religions met in Assisi, Italy to draft statements of concern. The level of activity heightened in the 1990s, stimulated in part by major world religious leaders such as Pope John Paul II and the "green" orthodox Patriarch Bartholomew, and by the Joint Appeal in Religion and Science in 1991. The Joint Appeal grew out of a collaboration the year before on an "Open Letter" from 34 internationally known concerned scientists in 1990 and a wide range of grassroots and para-denominational groups.

As you can see, our current level of awareness builds on a long but little known history of trying to raise awareness within religious communities and denominations. Many of the key voices that called us to the task and inspired action were faculty at seminaries who had a clear sense that we needed to educate future religious leaders for the task. Many of these visionary figures would meet in San Diego nearly two decades later to continue their call for environmental awareness. But despite the efforts of these committed scholars and activists, in the 90's, little was happening at most seminaries to reflect the awakening sense among religious leaders and people of faith.

At that time, Rick Clugston and Dieter Hessel, working with leaders in theological education and ecology, headed up the strategic initiative, Theological Education to Meet the Environmental Challenge (TEMEC). The conferences, workshops and lead institutions of this effort helped to produce the next generation of faculty and religious leaders around the country. Through TEMEC and the work of David Rhoads at Lutheran Theological School at Chicago (LTSC), the organization Web of Creation was created to be a clearinghouse of information for seminaries and congregations interested in the many dimensions of "greening." Web of Creation is still active today and an important resource for this work.

Now, as the news of climate change grows ever more perilous, the kind of systemic change envisioned by eco-theologians and TEMEC alike is only starting to happen. Many of the lead institutions slipped from their commitment once the early visionary leaders retired. Others, such as LTSC, continued to slowly build on that foundation so that LTSC now proudly proclaims itself as a green seminary in a green zone. Taking another innovative path to "green" is the Interdenominational Theological Center in Atlanta; "theoecology," as they term it, is part of their strategic plan and their President's message. But these are the exceptions, rather than the rule. When one surveys the landscape of seminaries, theological schools and divinity schools, very few can lay claim to being very green or sustainable institutions. Even many of those that are making efforts to incorporate eco-justice and sustainability into their curriculum and practices have not sufficiently put the environment front and center in their mission statement. For example, precious few have featured their environmental efforts on their websites. This all adds up to the need for a new focus on integrating eco-justice and sustainability throughout theological education.

## THE GREEN SEMINARY INITIATIVE

Building on the work of TEMEC and the Web of Creation, the Green Seminary Initiative was launched in November 2007 to reinvigorate an interfaith effort to infuse theological education with a commitment to a sustainable earth community. This initiative to "green" seminaries is premised on two convictions:

The first is that the religious community has a unique and significant calling to turn back human-caused environmental destruction. We are charged with bringing all of creation into health and wholeness. This task is central to the call of justice that issues from the Jewish, Christian and Muslim scriptures. Religious communities express thanks for God's creation. We remember that we are called to serve and preserve the earth. We participate in God's covenant with Noah and all living things, reminding ourselves that everything in creation was important enough to God to be saved, and that this covenant is not just with humans. We recognize our own human failing in our vocation to care for creation and to live in a sustainable global community. We gather to show reverence for the beauty and grieve the destruction. Together, we confront the spiritual crisis and reorient our hearts and minds to simpler, sustainable and just lives. Together, we work toward a vision of a renewed creation.

It is the task of religious leaders of today and tomorrow to help all people of faith and spirit live more fully in this vision. As Larry Rasmussen commented at the San Diego forum, "The ecological reformation has spiritual, moral, technological, and systemic dimensions, and the challenge for theological education is to re-think the faith so as to render it Earth-honoring and justice-centered for the whole community of life, biosphere and atmosphere together." It is important for all of us to pronounce the eco-justice aspects of this work, so that going green is not just about energy efficiency and new technologies.

The second conviction underpinning the Initiative is that seminaries and theological schools should provide religious leaders with the tools necessary to lead their congregations, communities and organizations in meeting their unique call. Specifically, we need a creation-centered education that provides the theological, scriptural, spiritual and ethical bases of creation care and eco-justice. We need to understand the depth of the challenges inherent to addressing the ecological crisis, and we need to understand the breadth of its reach — especially its impact upon the least among us. Few are as well positioned as seminaries and theological schools to lead the way to a more sustainable and just society that values a healthy planet.

This task will take theological education to new places, to widen even further its domain. As biologist and evangelical leader Cal DeWitt explains, "An important aspect of moving upward in theology and theological education is the need to integrate across understanding of the workings of the biosphere, the ethical underpinnings of a flourishing human society, and the applications of these toward right living and practice."

## SPECIFICS

The goal is for schools and congregations to incorporate care for all parts of creation into the identity and mission of each institution such that it becomes an integral part of its very ethos. In order to do this, schools and congregations will need to focus on the following program areas: curriculum, worship, sustainable building, grounds and institutional practices, community life and personal discipleship, and public ministry.

## *Curriculum*

Through education, seminaries can develop foundational and elective courses to equip each graduate with the intellectual and practical tools they will need. There is substantial environmental scholarship available now in all areas of the theological curriculum; many websites, such as www.webofcreation.org and the American Academy of Religion syllabus project, provide sample syllabi and other resources.

But teaching toward a sustainable and greener future will require more than simply retooling the curriculum that already exists. It also necessitates teaching students to pay attention to the more-than-human natural world, both in its beauty and grandeur and in its polluted and degraded state. We have too long operated on the assumption that what happens within our church and seminary walls is what is most important to our students and our faith traditions. But remember, Jesus and Moses were both experts at ministry outdoors!

Greening seminaries will also require incorporating science and economics more squarely within the curriculum. Students should be able to understand the enormity of the environmental crisis in specific, metric terms, and to think through ways we can envision the whole of creation renewed and transformed. Outside lecturers and half-to-whole-day workshops and classes by those already working in the field can help fill in gaps in a seminary faculty's expertise. Informative and transformative films such as *Renewal* and *In the Light of Reverence* can augment classroom teaching. Students might participate in field education experiences through immersion experiences, supervised ministry with green congregations, and internship projects with grassroots religious environmental organizations. Through this work, green seminaries will become centers of scholarship on creation-related topics, especially as they make the link between the environment and a just and sustainable world that is central to our faith traditions.

## Worship

Through worship, faculty, staff and students come together as a community to celebrate God's presence in creation, to worship with all living things and to remember the call to justice for all of creation that echoes forth from our traditions and scriptures. Worship also affords opportunities for restoring our relationship with creation through spiritual experience, praise, confession, pardon, petition and taking the church outdoors. Resources for bringing creation care into worship are offered by the Web of Creation, the National Council of Churches' Eco-Justice (www.nccecojustice. org), and in David Rhoads' volume, *Earth and Word*, which contains sample sermons from a wealth of eco-theologians and activists.

## Sustainable Building, Maintenance and Practices

Through sustainable building practices, facility and grounds maintenance, seminaries can serve as models for their students and communities. This kind of commitment to sustainability will function as a very visible laboratory for improving our environmental footprints. From the conservation of water, paper and energy, to supporting local growers and living wages, there are many ways to model sustainable behavior. Duke Divinity School's new refectory is an excellent example: They buy locally grown products, serve organic foods, support fair trade, offer a living wage to employees and recycle as much as possible. Another Methodist school, Candler School of Theology, will soon have two LEED-certified buildings; the Episcopal Church's General Theological School has a new geo-thermal heating and cooling system, as does Associate Mennonite Biblical Seminary, where other changes are taking place such as waterless urinals and rain gardens. Many schools, such as Drew Theological School and LTSC have installed automatic sensor lights and water fixtures, and more efficient lights and heating. They have also purchased 100% recycled paper, banned pesticides, planted native species, changed eating and drinking utensils to biodegradable and compostable, and examined the food and beverages served in terms of what is sustainable and fairly traded. Wesley Seminary has also made significant adjustments in its buildings and grounds as well as its dining services. For example, all eggs served at the refectory are now certified cage-free. Small or large, the aggregate effect of these choices is a dramatically lowered carbon footprint and an unquantifiable ripple effect in their student communities.

Many resources exist to show, at the institutional level, how to model best practices in the office and the refectory. The Association for the Advancement of Sustainability in Higher Education (AASHE) is an excellent information clearing house, as are a variety of regional consortiums. By transforming their own institutional practices, seminaries and theological schools can practice what we hope they preach, and also offer on-the-ground practical instruction on all aspects of creation-friendly buildings and grounds.

## Community Life, Personal Discipleship and Public Ministry

Our vision for environmental scholarship reaches into community life and personal discipleship. Faculty, staff and students alike should be encouraged to adopt personal and communal lifestyles that are simple and light on the earth. In addition to the institutional practices mentioned above, food services, transportation, recycling, and less consumer-oriented lifestyles are all part of honoring and respecting creation and bringing about a healthy, just and sustainable global community. Once their awareness is raised, whether it is about disposable coffee cups and water bottles, or reusing paper and recycling, students become teachers in their home congregations, families and communities.

Seminaries can promote this awareness in the broader religious and world community by offering conferences, workshops and retreats and by providing printed and online resources. There are countless opportunities to partner with religious organizations that exist specifically to address environmental issues, such as Green-Faith and Earth Ministry, or the various state Interfaith Power and Light groups. These are key avenues of outreach, especially when we remember that theological education has a wide constituency, including local laity, those already ordained or serving the community or church, or those involved with camp and conference retreat ministries. There are many who have finished their theological education, or who are already trained in environmental studies, who long to put the two together. For instance, Drew, in addition to offering a doctorate of ministry in Environmental Ministries and Ecological Spirituality, has partnered with GreenFaith to give continuing-education credit to laity and ordained clergy through their GreenFaith Fellowship program.

Christianity started as a religion out of doors, and it is often at camp and retreat settings that people have significant encounters with God and the sacred. Unfortunately, all too often they go back to settings where they fear admitting the depth and significance of encountering the sacred in nature, Perhaps they will be labeled pagan, or accused of worshipping the creation and not the creator (a charge particularly frequent in more conservative settings).

I often feel the real reason I am asked to speak on panels is to let people know that it is okay to experience God in nature; that the tradition and the scriptures will back them up – my credibility as a professor at a theological school doesn't hurt either. In the audience, I see smiles and nods of acknowledgement, and in workshops and classes, people will often admit to a significant encounter with the sacred while in nature – something they tell very few people. For camp and retreat workers, it is often their own deep sense of God in the creation that has brought them to work in this kind of ministry, and it is at camps that many feel the first call to ministry. Religious camps and retreat centers, where the house of worship is outdoors, are significant components to a creation-caring ministry. The students whom I have taught through Drew's Common Ground program (which certifies camp and retreat personnel around the common ground of earth and a diverse human community) have been very enthusiastic and receptive to the full message of creation care.

Again, let me refer to the Web of Creation website as a wonderful resource to help the greening of our seminaries. They provide information for students, faculty and administrators, and report extensively on what other seminaries are doing to promote care of creation. They even provide a step-by-step how-to guide to greening a seminary, including a list called, "What Every Seminarian Should Learn about Caring for Creation."

The ecological challenges that face the world are difficult, imminent and of paramount importance. Religious institutions can play an enormous part in addressing those challenges. John Cobb reminds us of just how important this work is:

> To seek to save the world from the self-destruction on which it is now embarked does not mean to turn away from issues of peace, justice, and inclusivism. It does mean to approach these issues with deep consciousness of their relations to one another and to the fate of the earth. It is only when they are approached in isolation from one another that they can lead to fragmentation of progressive action. The concern to save the

*earth can provide the unity which too often progressives have lacked. Seminaries have resources for displaying this holistic approach to the critical needs of the world.*

If theological education takes its role in training effective religious leaders seriously, religious institutions will be in a far better place to help transform lives and lifestyles for real, sustainable ecological change.

18

SR. PAT NAGLE

CONGREGATION OF SISTERS, SERVANTS OF THE IMMACULATE HEART OF MARY

PORTLAND, OREGON

# On Our Way Home

"Often, I would catch a glimpse of a Banyan tree, tenderly dressed in a skirt as a sign of its sacredness. On a very visceral level, the Balinese people knew of their intimate connection to all of life, and they viewed all of life as sacred."

It is a privilege for me to be here in the midst of our earth community right now. Though it is a dark time — the diminishment of the ecosystems of earth, the loss of species, stark poverty, wars and fractured relationships all over — it is also a time of great hope, as so much work is being done to restore earth and to remember the unity of our One Earth Community. My sense of hope and privilege might best be expressed in the words of Joanna Macy, who said in a recent article,

> To us is granted the privilege of being on hand, to take part, if we choose, in the Great Turning to a just and sustainable society. We can

*let life work through us, enlisting all our strength, wisdom and courage, so that life itself can continue. (from "Gratitude: Where Healing the Earth Begins,"* Shambala Sun, *Nov. 2007)*

Thus I am committed to engaging in this process, one that I believe is sacred, and I am moved to be and do all that I can. I look back in wonder at the events in my life that have opened my heart, enabling me to hear and serve this call.

I was born in Lewiston, Idaho, located on the banks of the Snake River in the Columbia River Watershed and the Cascadia Bioregion. In the early years of my life I lived in Pullman, Washington, nestled among the rolling wheat fields of Palouse County. I spent my summers on the water, in a house boat on Priest Lake, or in the forests of Western Washington State with my father, a professor of Forestry. When not among the trees or floating along the water, I strolled the endless shore of Long Beach, Washington. Always, I have felt an intimate bond with earth, with the silent, strong evergreens in the Pacific Northwest, the vast, deep blue waters of the Pacific Ocean and the magnetic Cascade sentinels. I have said to friends that the spacious and strong-yet-fragile geography of the Wild West is my internal geography. This intuitive stance of kinship, this participative bonding, has been a source of consolation, comfort and encouragement in times when life's surprises seemed too much for me.

When my father died on the day I returned home to the West after being in ministry in the Midwest, grief ripped me apart. I had moved to California, where I was studying, and would travel time and time again to Muir Wood and walk through the giant redwoods. I felt protected amongst the slivers of light breaking through the canopy of darkness, and began to reweave my life. In later years, as I struggled with the shocking diagnosis of breast cancer, I would sit for long periods under the tulip tree in our backyard. This bonding, this sense of interdependence, shared fragility and impulse towards life, served as a kind of container for me. And thus it is this belief, that I am one with all of life, that still serves as my inner guide and invites me to put my energies at the service of the whole earth.

For me, this earth is a sacred community, and I am each day invited into a relationship of mutuality, respecting all others and the unique manifestation of the divine each one carries within. I am moved to provide, to the best of my ability, an environment for the other to thrive and reveal the fullness of divine life within. If I were to name this grounding, it would be a nascent knowing that we are one sacred community of life: How I am and what I do affects the on-going expression of the divine in this community. All is one.

## Our Garden

This belief guided my work with Earth Home Ministries, a community garden program in Oakland, California. From 1989 to 2002, I had the opportunity to work with Sister Sharon Joyer, Sister of Notre Dame de Namur, along with many neighbors and colleagues, to reclaim a sense of belonging to self, each other, to earth, to neighborhood and the larger community. We wanted to create a feeling of home and restore a sense of place, motivated by our belief in the sacredness of all life and appreciation for its diverse expressions. We were moved by the many stories we heard from members of the local community about violence, loneliness and alienation in the neighborhood. We experienced sadness from the carjacking and murder of a neighbor, as well as deep dismay from the multiple drug-related shoot-outs nearby. Neighbors lived in fear and isolation from one another. We decided to open our home as a safe place for all of us to come together.

We shared stories as we all enjoyed the harvests from our backyard garden. Soon, you could feel the universal desire to reclaim our lives, our security and our place; neighbors began sharing slips of plants. Earth became the place where we could meet around common interests and feel safe and comforted. In time, our neighborhood community garden was established and served as an amazing laboratory for us all. We learned about our interconnectedness with all of life and about cooperative, respectful living with peaceful conflict resolution. The garden provided a meeting place where folks of all ages and cultures would gather and remember forgotten connections with one another, with plants, insects, sun and moon. Often, we were inspired to create rituals to help us integrate the experiences into our separate lives. With the gardeners, we blessed the seeds before planting and celebrated the harvest with the cultural rainbow of the neighborhood. As we cultivated our garden, so too did we cultivate and give expression to our commitment to earth-based service. And as we worked the soil and watered our seedlings, we helped ameliorate some of those feelings of alienation, insecurity and vulnerability.

## RISK, FAITH AND TRANSFORMATION

My life and service have also been shaped by my community of Sisters: Sisters, Servants of the Immaculate Heart of Mary (SSIHM) of Monroe, Michigan. With them, I align my personal beliefs to those of a larger group that works cooperatively for a more peaceful, just and sustainable world. Since our beginnings in 1845, our guiding vision has been to participate in the liberating mission of Jesus, to discern the areas of oppression and to put our energies toward their service. Throughout the years we have gathered to re-interpret this founding energy and the Gospel teachings in light of the changing needs of the times. We are committed to working for the eradication of the causes of injustice, and for racial and gender equality. In the late '80s, informed by our studies of feminist spirituality, prayers, and the emerging new worldview – one, interdependent community of life – we set out to clarify our growing understanding of interdependence and unity with all creation. In the mid '90s we affirmed our corporate belief that the earth was among the oppressed, and so committed to setting our energies toward the service of the whole earth community. We consider the earth to be a living organism, with a right to thrive and flourish. To the SSIHM community, this commitment to sustainability is a moral mandate for 21st century. We strive to look at our lives and our decisions through this lens.

As life is never without its irony and symbolism, while grappling with our great commitment to the whole of the earth and our respect for its diminishing resources, we faced a decision about our own motherhouse building, where our retired and infirm sisters live. The old depression-era building was structurally sound, but its systems – heating, cooling, lighting and plumbing – were crumbling. Should we renovate or tear it down? Either way, we had to be guided by our commitment to sustainability. Through a lengthy process, in which all were invited to participate to the extent that she could, we decided to renovate under principles of green design. As you can imagine, this was a huge financial investment for our community of aging women. In the end, our faith that moved us to "risk deeds our hearts could never dream" (a beloved phrase and aspiration from SSIHM's traditions). We knew the risk was worth it (despite our trepidations), and restored and transformed this little bit of earth into a center for sustainable living that would impact our lives and generations to come. It is now our gift to the wider community, and hopefully a catalyst for our own continued transformation.

These powerful, personal experiences with the communal process for the sustainable stewardship of the earth have invited me to face my own limitations and vulnerabilities squarely, and embrace them as guides for the growth of the "Kindom." As a person of faith, in the light of the of earth's suffering and very diminishment, I must take risks to live differently, to carefully examine what I do and do not need, and to see more clearly the manner in which I relate to the community of life. I ask myself: Do I relate as subject to subject, or as subject to object? How much is enough? It is this kind of engagement that keeps the process of life emerging.

And it is always emerging.

## ON TO BALI

Fast forward to late spring of 2007. I was invited to join a delegation for the World Council of Churches at the 13th United Nations Framework Convention on Climate Change in Bali, Indonesia. Though a cautious traveler, I actually leapt with my heart and body to accept the invitation! The opportunity was surely a moment of grace, moving me from my intuitive stance of oneness with all to a cooperative engagement with the world on the most pressing environmental need of our time: crafting a global response to climate change, its effect on earth and, particularly, the most vulnerable ones in the earth community.

As co-chair of Oregon Interfaith Power and Light Advisory Committee, I have the opportunity to meet with people of different faiths and spiritual traditions. I listen to their concerns regarding climate change and observe their courageous, creative responses to the issue. Now, I could take these experiences to the global community. My journey to Bali would prove to refine my heart and my life's work, as I became immersed with Balinese culture and spirituality and worked across international boundaries for this issue we all hold in common.

My companion on the plane from San Francisco was a young man on his way home to Vietnam. He had left there at age four and now, 16 years later, was returning. As we talked, we noticed that our journeys had something in common: home. He said to me, "You're concerned about home too, huh, and caring for it." This is indeed the foundation for all our work in restoring health to our earth. When we parted ways in Taipei, we assured one another of our shared hopes and love for home in all its forms: earth, Vietnam, Oregon...

The Indonesian people brought this idea to great clarity. As I drove into Bali I saw people gathered around shrines, sitting in a circle with offerings, enjoying the company of one another, and calling upon the sacred, which is ever present in their lives. As I came to know the Balinese Hindu peoples, I was moved by this constant attention to the sacred. Shrines and rituals were everywhere. I studied their yearly calendar of moon cycles carefully. Each day invited certain practices in relation to the elements, earth, air, fire and water. Farmers performed specific rituals on certain days for planting their rice or other crops. There are temples at every main juncture, near the waters, in the midland areas and amongst the mountainous terraced regions. Often, I would catch a glimpse of a Banyan tree, tenderly dressed in a skirt as a sign of its sacredness. On a very visceral level, the Balinese people knew of their intimate connection to all of life, and they viewed all of life as sacred. Acknowledging this with profound gratitude and simplicity was central for them. I wondered about this and if the fact that the Balinese Hindu people live in an area so influenced by a range of active volcanic peaks and frequent earthquakes had any influence. They seemed to know that their very survival depended on nurturing this connection to the sacred, moment by moment, in all the routines of daily life.

At the Bali Convention, over 180 nations gathered to share stories and to find an answer to the crisis of climate change, the moral issue of our time. The prevailing ethos at the Convention was that no matter how critical things are, we who are present now on earth have an opportunity and a responsibility to make a difference. In this spirit, I heard from a representative of the People's Republic of Bangladesh of the great work there in an area particularly vulnerable to flooding. Folks on the local level are educating rural people about the importance of planting trees to hold the soil in times of floods. A youth brigade was formed in another area and has organized 4800 households to plant coco-nut and guava saplings. In Papua New Guinea, the Eco-Forestry Forum has organized for the protection of the forests. They see the forest as providers of life-sustaining services like fuel, food and shelter. They know the trees are the lungs of the earth and see their destruction as a moral issue. They have therefore brought suit against foreign logging entities and have lobbied with their own government for the practice of sustainable forestry. Their teams go into rural villages to educate at the very local level and provide a voice for them.

Nonetheless, response to climate change is slow work. In Bali we grappled with questions for the world community: What is our responsibility to assist those affected by climate change? What do we do to mitigate our own part in the destruction of the earth and the build-up of $CO_2$ emissions? What is our response?

Those of us from the World Council of Churches delegation said that we do have a moral responsibility to respond, and that we need to call upon the wisdom of our faith traditions. For centuries, our traditions have been founded upon values such as "love your neighbor," and "care for the common good." We called for the deliberations at the UN Convention to be guided by these principles, as well as the "values of equality, solidarity, justice human development and environmental conservation." (from the World Council of Churches statement in Bali, Dec. 2007)

## ONE SACRED COMMUNITY

In the months since returning from Bali, I have had countless opportunities to share my experience with many from different faith/spiritual traditions. Each time, I revisit my early years amid the trees and along the rivers of the Northwest, and reexamine the beliefs that have formed me and become operative in my life. Faith, for me, is a particular kind of consciousness — the consciousness of God, the divine, as loving and caring and at the heart of all life. Faith is more about how I behave than about holding on to certain precepts. Since I do believe that God's life pulsates in and beyond all of life, then for me, all life is revelatory of God. As in the case of Jesus, and other figures of wisdom from each tradition, this union, this connection to God, the holy one, is the center from which my life and my actions flow. Therefore, I seek to live my life in this place of union and to live in such a way as to support the continued expression of the sacred.

In other words, I am responsible for seeing that my life and my actions help foster an environment that invites the fullest expression of divine life in the others. The evidence is all around of the seriousness of climate change and of the violence and the broken relationships in our homes and communities on many levels. Each one of us – and I'll start with myself – are invited by our creator each day to reexamine our lifestyles, to name our operative beliefs and balance them with our actions. We do this always holding in our hearts the image of earth, our one sacred community of life.

I have a friend who reminds me frequently of the invitation to keep focused on the big love, and so I'll pay the favor forward and remind you too. Allow me once more to quote Joanna Macy:

> We have received an inestimable gift. To be alive in this beautiful, self-organizing universe – to participate in the dance of life with senses to perceive it, lungs that breathe it, organs that draw nourishment from it – is a wonder beyond words. It is an extraordinary privilege to be accorded a human life, with self-reflexive consciousness that brings awareness of our own actions and the ability to make choices. It lets us choose to take part in the healing of our world. (from "Gratitude")

May this be the grounding of our lives and our work as we strengthen our bonds with one another, with all life, set our faces to the sun, and move on with courage, wonder and fearlessness to create a more just, sustainable, compassionate earth community.

## 19

MARY EVELYN TUCKER
YALE UNIVERSITY
NEW HAVEN, CT

# Renewing Hope

"What has emerged in the last dozen years is a growing awareness of the important role of religion, spirituality, values and ethics in environmental studies and environmental action."

❧

A midst all the challenging environmental news of our time, we are in need of causes for rejoicing, for continuing, for renewing hope. The work of so many people, engaged scholars and theologians, along with religious environmentalists, is a large part of this tapestry of renewing hope — for there is emerging a new field of religion and ecology within academia, along with a potent new force of religious environmental activism in the United States and around the world.

While religions have been late in responding to environmental issues, and despite the historic problematic issues often connected to religions, they are clearly gaining traction. This is because they have the ability to change from within and to spark change without. These are not static institutions. Religions have inspired movements for social change, as they did in the 19th century with the abolitionist movement and in the 20th century with civil rights, workers rights, and women's rights. In each case, as the moral dimension of these issues became more evident, shifts in attitudes and behavior occurred. It is important to note that, in addition to the movement of established religions into environmental concerns, there are many people who are inspired to be engaged in ecological work from a broad spiritual perspective that is not necessarily associated with a particular institutional religion. Both religious and spiritual environmental activism need to be encouraged and supported.

This is what is happening in the environmental movement now, as it is becoming clearer that human values and spiritual perspectives have an important role to play in creating pathways toward a sustainable future. Indeed, many of the early environmentalists such as John Muir and Henry David Thoreau were themselves deeply inspired by the spiritual dimensions of nature. Now every major religion has statements on the environment, eco-justice offices have been set up, both clergy and lay are becoming active, eco-theologians are publishing widely, the greening of seminaries is being encouraged, and a whole new field of study and teaching is emerging in colleges and universities.

Religious leaders and laity, in particular, are now addressing climate change. In the Christian community, the World Council of Churches has been working on this issue for many years, and more recently the Evangelical community has been speaking out on the effect of climate change on the poor. The Interfaith Power and Light movement has sparked hundreds of churches and synagogues to change their light bulbs and reduce their carbon footprint. In September 2007, the Ecumenical Patriarch Bartholomew organized a symposium in Greenland to highlight the effects of climate change. The US Catholic Bishops have issued a statement on global warming and the Pope has also spoken about this as a moral issue.

With these efforts becoming more visible, there is a growing recognition that despite the problems with religion there is also great promise for addressing environmental issues. While religions may be dogmatic and intolerant and can contribute to conflict and violence, they can also be a source of significant charitable efforts, the champions of the poor or downtrodden, and spokespersons for justice against oppressive powers. This is true for the traditions of the West, as well as of Asia and of indigenous traditions.

At present, religions can play a key role in sparking the moral transformation toward a sustainable and sustaining future. This is because they shape cultural values and are vessels of moral authority. Many of them have large numbers of adherents, and in raising awareness of the environmental crisis as an ethical and spiritual issue, they can make a significant difference.

The striking news is not only that this work is receiving more attention in the press, but that it is also being encouraged by scientists and policy-makers. They too are calling for the involvement of religious communities in environmental issues. Indeed, this has directly affected the field of study of religion and ecology, for it was in this spirit that my husband, John Grim, and I were invited to come to Yale to teach in the joint degree program between the

School of Forestry and Environmental Studies and the Divinity School. There is a new realization at Yale and beyond that religious values are indispensable partners in finding environmental solutions. The academic field of religion and ecology is helping religious traditions reformulate their teachings and their ethics to embrace not only human-centered concerns but also human-earth relations. For example, the Biblical notion of human "dominion" over the earth is being reexamined by Jewish and Christian theologians; the concept of stewardship is becoming central instead, and this encourages environmental action. This is an example of just one aspect of a mutually beneficial interaction between theological and scholarly reflection working alongside religious environmental activism. Theory and practice are transforming one another.

## WHY RELIGION AND ECOLOGY?

For me, coming to Yale is part of a longer journey into the conjunction of religion and ecology. It began some 35 years ago when I taught at a university in Japan. There, I fell in love with Asia's varied cultural traditions and art, Zen gardens and flower arrangement — along with the spectacular beauty of the countryside and the mountains. I sank into another kind of appreciation for nature, wild and cultivated, both in the ancient city of Kyoto and in the agricultural cycles of rice-growing.

When I went to Japan in 1973, a few years after the first Earth Day, environmental problems were still at the periphery of most people's awareness. In the United States the liberating movements of the 1960s, for civil rights and women's rights, were emerging. The Vietnam War, which had divided the country so bitterly, was still being waged, while the Watergate scandal cast a long shadow over domestic politics. I needed distance from the upheavals of the war, having spent my college years in Washington. So for nearly two years I was fully immersed in a Japanese university, in a southern provincial city that had very little exposure to foreigners. It changed my life forever as I tried to understand the very different worldviews and values of Japanese society, culture and religions.

On my way back to the United States, I traveled through Southeast Asia and India. I stopped in Saigon to visit a friend who was working in an orphanage. This was my first encounter with the environmental effects of war; the devastation of "Agent Orange" was evident across the countryside, and so was its subsequent effect on people. The impact of seeing this war-ravaged country a few months before South Vietnam fell was almost too much to bear.

This was only the beginning. I have closely watched what has happened to the environment in Asia over the last three decades and the change is almost inconceivable. The Asia I traveled through in the 1970s was worlds apart from where it is today. The cities of Taipei and Bangkok, Seoul and Delhi, while poor, were livable then, before rapid and relentless modernization hit like a great tidal wave, engulfing everything in its path. In many cities, like Beijing and Bangalore, the tsunami of modernization has wiped away whole neighborhoods and the rapid reconstruction and growth of car culture has left relentless air pollution. The search for modern economic progress has dammed the Yangtze River in southern China, and the Narmada River in Western India, in the largest engineering projects the world has ever seen, submerging ancient archaeological sites and uprooting millions of people. The environmental impact was so great that in both cases that the World Bank withdrew its funding. This "progress" came at a price for the people and the planet.

This wave of industrialization in India and China is changing the face of the earth and putting enormous pressure on ecosystems all over the world, as over two billion people struggle to gain the fruits of modernity and the promise of progress for themselves. Should they not too have electricity and cars, clean water and computers? How can one balance economic development and environmental protection under these circumstances? This is one of the most pressing issues of our global environmental crisis, involving the contested terrain of sustainable development and eco-justice.

With a concern, then, for both environmental degradation and the consequences for human flourishing, I asked myself, "How can I contribute to the discussions on the environment, not being a scientist or a policy-maker, but a historian of religions?" I realized that the world's religions might be an entryway. Religious traditions that shape human-and-earth relations could have a role to play in solving environmental problems. Moreover, it is clear that environmental ethics have a religious and cultural base and thus will be formulated differently in Asia than in the United States, or in Africa, or in Latin America, or China or India. And so we began to explore how these varied religious worldviews and ethical attitudes toward nature could be understood and then factored into concern and attention to the environment.

## THE HARVARD CONFERENCE SERIES ON WORLD RELIGIONS AND ECOLOGY

This thinking formed the basis of the Harvard conference series, from 1996-1998, that I organized with John Grim. The conference series also grew out of our many years of research in the world's religious traditions; John's work focused on the western religions and indigenous traditions, and mine concentrated on the Asian religions. We were especially fortunate to study with comprehensive and engaged scholars who were deeply involved with reformulating traditional values in modern contexts. They included Thomas Berry at Fordham, Theodore de Bary at Columbia and Tu Weiming at Harvard.

When John and I invited scholars of Confucianism and Buddhism to Harvard to explore the intersection of religion and ecology in the mid-1990s, this was still a new idea. It took some lengthy phone conversations to bring people on board and to overcome skepticism. After all, they were scholars of complex historical traditions, translators of ancient texts, and decoders of centuries-old commentaries. What could these specialized studies have to do with environmental problems emerging in Asia from rampant industrialization?

But the response was remarkable. Within a short period of time we had a full cadre of participants committed, coming from both North America and Asia. They wanted to bring their knowledge of these religious traditions to address the pressing issues facing contemporary Asia. However, there was a hitch: No foundations were interested in giving grants; it was such a novel idea for them that religions might actually have a role to play in environmental issues. Fortunately, with some persuasion, a few key foundations eventually supported the conference series and the ongoing work in this field.

The Harvard conference series on religion and ecology incorporated an acknowledgement of the problematic side of religions as well as recognition of the disjunction between religious traditions and modern environmental problems. The participants understood the historical and cultural divide between texts written in earlier periods for different ends and the ends we sought today. They worked within a process of retrieving texts and traditions, critically reevaluating them, and then reconstructing them for present circumstances. They underscored the gap between theory and practice, noting that textual passages that celebrate nature do not automatically lead to the protection of nature. Thus, there is an important dialogue that should occur between environmental historians and historians of religions to explore the interaction of intellectual ideas and practices in relation to actual environmental conditions. Moreover, the conference series and the ongoing work in the field have been both inter-religious and interdisciplinary, engaging scientists, economists and policy makers. It also brought together scholars and activists in an unusual intersection of theory and practice.

With the collaboration of some 800 scholars of religion and environmentalists, the ten conference and volumes were completed between 1996 and 2004. In addition, scholars have established groups in the American Academy of Religion on religion and ecology, and religion and animals. In the last decade, a new journal, *Worldviews*, was launched, along with a major international website (www.yale.edu/religionandecology). And in 1998, John and I founded the Forum on Religion and Ecology; the Canadian Forum on Religion and Ecology was established several years later.

## ENGAGED SCHOLARS AND RELIGIOUS ENVIRONMENTAL ACTIVISTS

I tell this origin story to illustrate several things: First, support for this work has grown despite great odds and endless uncertainty. Second, collaboration has been central to the Forum's work from the beginning. We built bridges across religious traditions and sought dialogue with other disciplines studying environmental issues. Third, scholars of religion and religious environmental activists participated together throughout the conference series. This is also reflected in the Harvard conference volumes and the website, which features case studies of "engaged projects." While the alliance of academics and activists may appear unusual at times, it has proven synergistic beyond expectation. Ideas and action cross-fertilize one another, sparking new forms of engaged scholarship and reflective action for long-term change.

What has emerged in the last dozen years is a growing awareness of the important role of religion, spirituality, values and ethics in environmental studies and environmental action. We can describe this as two wings: the *field* of religion and ecology, and the *force* of religious environmentalism. The first I will call "religious ecology" for the sake of contrast and clarification. I use the term "ecology" self-consciously, for it has not always been understood the same way across the board. As I mean it, ecology is the interconnected study of nature, species and dynamic ecosystems, from scientific and ecological perspectives, but also including humans. For example, theologians in this area are contributing new understandings of incarnation as the Logos of the entire universe, of sacraments as containing sacred elements of nature, of ritual as reflecting the great seasonal cycles, and of ethics as embracing eco-justice. The theological formulation of this is expanding the traditions and grounding religious practice in a larger sense of significance.

I use the term "religious environmentalism" to describe the activism of a religious nature that calls for protection or restoration of the environment in a variety of ways, ranging from river cleanup and tree planting to changing light bulbs and reducing waste. Religious environmentalism, from grassroots activism to religious leadership, models sustainability for people, builds eco-justice in communities, and links humans to the earth in new and creative ways. It is emerging in projects of all the world's religions.

It is becoming clearer from this shared work of study and practice that the world's religions have certain common values in relation to nature. These might be described as the six Rs: reverence, respect, restraint, redistribution, responsibility and renewal. While there are clearly variations among religions with regard to the expression of these values, it is evident that religions worldwide are moving into their ecological phase. They can bring forth a profound *reverence* for earth as a sacred community of life. They can urge *respect* for the earth's myriad species and expand their ethics to include all life forms. They can call for *restraint* in the use of natural resources (and support for effective alternative technologies). They can advocate for equitable *redistribution* of wealth between rich and poor. They can acknowledge human *responsibility* in regard to the continuity of life and ecosystems that support life for future generations. Finally, they can be a source of *renewal* and hope in the midst of the deeply challenging environmental crisis we are facing both locally and globally.

## THE EMERGING ALLIANCE

Where does this leave us? I believe, with a sense of renewed hope regarding the emerging alliance of religion and ecology. That is because it is both a field and a force: a field growing within academia, which is trying to break down its "silo disciplines" and enter into an interdisciplinary conversation for a sustainable future;

and a force of empowerment on the ground and in religious institutions, for religious leaders and laity alike. We recognize that we draw from each other — the field of religious ecology and the force of religious environmentalism. We cannot do this work alone, but together, new synergies will arise of reformation and renaissance.

Some have called for an ecological reformation of religious traditions, and this is clearly underway, thanks to the efforts of so many people, scholars and activists alike. In addition, it is my hope that the pressing ecological and social needs of the larger earth community will call us to ignite an even broader ecological renaissance that will truly renew the face of the earth.

## 20

SR. GAIL WORCELO
GREEN MOUNTAIN MONASTERY
GREENSBORO, VERMONT

# A Monastery Cairn

"Throughout the ages and in various cultures many hands
have picked up stones, both literally and metaphorically, and
in a profound yet simple act have laid them down
for those who would follow."

Several months ago, during the formal Blessing of Green Mountain Monastery and the Dedication of our land as the Fr. Thomas Berry Sanctuary, our friend Sarah Taylor, author of *Green Sisters: A Spiritual Ecology*, referred to our monastery in her homily reflection as a cairn, pointing the way to a new evolutionary and cosmological consciousness.

Sarah said, "This Monastery points the way to a new era of mutually beneficial relations with the total sacred community of life. It reaches back to the bedrock of the Catholic tradition while forging that bedrock into its newest cosmological and planetary expression."

The word *cairn* has its origins in the Scottish-Gaelic language and refers to a mound of stones piled up as a marker. The ancient gesture of piling stones in a mound to mark a path or point the way through unfamiliar landscape is embedded in the DNA of our humanity.

Throughout the ages and in various cultures many hands have picked up stones, both literally and metaphorically, and in a profound yet simple act have laid them down for those who would follow.

Cairns are often found at borders or crossings to offer the traveler direction on what is usually a disorienting or precarious path. Oftentimes cairns grow or enlarge as each passing traveler adds a stone, as if to say to the next traveler, "Trust the Way" or "The path is made by walking." Coming across a cairn on a long and arduous journey gives one the sense that all is not lost.

Here at Green Mountain Monastery we are laying down some stone markers pointing the way through this time that scientists are calling the sixth mass extinction period in the history of the planet. While the other five were caused by natural occurrences such as climate or asteroids, this extinction moment is being caused by our human community. There is a movement in consciousness here at the monastery and around the world as we realize that we are living on a withering planet and are, ourselves, an endangered species on the edge of extinction. There is so much being lost and so much to lose!

Yet, even as our life support systems crumble, that ancient human gesture of laying down stones to mark the way seems to arise from the deep center of our human experience. A stone is placed here and there, another is added to the pile, each pointing to a new consciousness emerging around the planet that manifests in phrases such as "A Single Sacred Community," "Awakening into Oneness," "Mutually Interpenetrating," "A Planetary Community," "A Communion of Subjects," "Enlightened Consciousness," and so on, stone placed upon stone.

In response to the current situation, our mentor Thomas Berry says, "If the dynamics of the universe from the beginning shaped the course of the heavens, lighted the sun and formed the Earth, if this dynamism brought forth the continents...and finally brought us into being and guided us safely through turbulent centuries, there is reason to believe that this same guiding process is what has awakened in us at the present moment." (from *The Great Work: Our Way Into the Future*)

In this 21st century, we have no maps as we make our way into the future; there are only cairns to guide us. Here in Vermont, we are shaping a Monastery Cairn that is integral with itself and the planet at every level, from catching the energy of the sun with our solar panels to deepening our own interior consciousness so that our awakening into oneness folds into the entire evolutionary process and helps bring it forward.

As you take your own journey, look for the cairns that lead the way, that will give you direction when you feel lost or can't find your path in the darkness. As you pass, leave your own stone and think of the many who will come after you. The Green Mountain Monastery is one cairn on the path, as are each of the congregations and organizations represented in this book and all the gatherings of people of faith for the good of the Earth — we are beautiful markers of hope, scattered around the planet, but leading the way to our future as a Single Sacred Community.

ॐ

## A Prayer Stone

I carry this prayer stone
And lay it down as a gesture of care for all
Beings of the future.
This stone, my heart prayer
Solid and steady, firm and resolved
Becomes part of a holy cairn,
A chapel of stones reaching to the heavens
To light the way.

# Who, If Not Us?
# Looking Ahead

༄

T hose are my friends that you have heard from. They are the greatest gift to me and my ministry that God could have provided. It was not my intention to make more friends. It was not my intention to unite religious leaders. Nor was it a goal of this ministry or mission, but I learned something: When one starts a project with a single goal in mind, one must stay open for profound and unexpected consequences. Not only has the message of environmental stewardship resonated with millions of people of faith in America and climate change climbed to the top on the ladder of concerns, but these "friends" of mine are all in agreement about saving the very thing that was put into place to sustain us. The Earth.

*Love God, Heal Earth* came about in the most unusual way. I had considered writing a book some day, but it was scheduled to be twenty years from now and more of a memoir than a collection of essays from courageous religious leaders. When I got the call from St. Lynn's Press and an offer to help to organize and pull together what, indeed, has proved to be an important piece of literature, I was startled. How many times have I heard people say, "I've written this important book and I cannot find a publisher." For me, who hadn't intended a book in the first place, this was puzzling. On the other end of the phone was a publisher with vision, and two skillful editors who were offering to help. Could I trust them, was the first question. If it is so hard to get a book published, could this be a legitimate offer? The time is NOW they said. A movement to switch to a clean energy economy is underway and the Interfaith Power and Light Campaign is one of the leaders. Religion is playing an important role and we want to publish the documentation of this movement. I knew that they were right about the movement and that religion was an important player. In fact, without religious voices addressing climate protection, the changes that need to be made won't make it to second base. If these strangers on the phone agreed with that, then I was listening. After some time to think about it, but still with some hesitation, I agreed. I entered a world that was and still is very new to me. I began pulling together a list of people I thought might be willing to contribute. The proof of the readiness for the word to be heard is that NO ONE said NO.

Our collective work has grounded us (literally) in a collaborative effort to help save the Creation from irreversible destruction. Some of us have worked closer together than others, but we are united in our effort, and the extraordinary thing is the depth of solidarity among diverse religious on the matter of climate protection. I would not ever have met Joel Hunter, Gerald Durley, Richard Cizik, Fred Small or Andrea Cohen-Kiener or any of the others, had it not been for our devotion to this work. These religious leaders have entered my life, not because we share life styles, workplaces, sports activities, social events, or are parents of children the same age. We didn't go to school together and we all come from different parts of the country and vastly different backgrounds and educations. And yet we are standing in solidarity, fighting for the same cause. Each of us in our deepest place has given in to a passion that touches us more profoundly than any of the other causes. We love each other for two reasons: We have a shared purpose, and we need each other to be successful. Never has there been competition, or "my religion says it better than yours." In most cases those traditional ways of doing business have been left behind and I think it is because we see the disaster on the horizon. We have to work together. Cooperation is the key here, not competition. We all know the consequences if we cannot convince our followers (whatever religion) to see and accept responsibility to save ourselves from ourselves.

I have been an environmentalist for over 25 years and argued for many causes. I have witnessed competition among environmental groups as to which one can take credit for a victory in court – who played the more important role in getting legislation passed to raise automobile efficiency standards. My friends and religious leaders around the world may get to that some time down the road, but today we are united. It is a joy to have this side benefit to our work and it has made moving forward easier than it might have been otherwise. When Christians, Muslims, Buddhist, Jews, Quakers, Unitarians, Mormons and Evangelicals can come together to save Creation, we make a giant step toward peace in the world as well. As M.E. Tucker says, there will not be peace in the world until everyone has access to clean air and clean water. The Nobel

Peace Prize committee made it clear that human-induced climate change will be a peace and security issue for the 21st century.

Slow to respond to the issue, the religious community is playing catch-up, but with enormous success and influence. We bring *hope* – which is a crucial ingredient of faith – to the never-ending doomsday message from the environmental community.

I am also fascinated by the similarities between the stories of dawning environmental awareness; some would call it consciousness, others might say metanoia. Several contributors had an early connection with the Creator in nature that stayed with them as they moved through the secular, often quite disconnected, world. This personal experience of the divine among the trees, mountains and streams of childhood leads directly to an understanding of creation care in adulthood. Pastor Pat Watkins, Sister Pat Nagle, and Mohamad Chakaki, for example, argue quite persuasively that for many, our connection to nature, to God's creation, has been fractured. To heal the Earth, as they see it, we must heal this rift in our very souls.

Others came to creation care through their commitment to civil rights and social justice. One of the key ingredients in Rabbi Cohen-Kiener's coming-to-wisdom was her feminist scholarship and its analysis of social inequities. Reverend Gerald Durley describes making the connection between human rights and the preservation of our Earth as he was watching the film, *The Great Warming*: "[A]bout half way through the movie I began to see, feel and understand something that was so real and truly *was* destroying all human, plant and animal life, equally. Suddenly, I remembered the words, 'Let there be light,' and the light of awareness flashed brilliantly in my mind...."

In a very different way, Imam Salie brings these concepts together in his descriptions of South Africa, a land of great natural beauty that has also seen centuries of suffering and struggle for human freedom. With this as an integral part of his consciousness, Salie follows the example of the Prophet Mohammad, as Muslims are called to do, in pursuit of justice for his fellow humans and the Earth, together.

Where I see contrast among our contributors is in the vision each has for the future. More than one quotes Proverbs 29:18, "Where there is no vision, people perish." In the Bible there are glimpses of a new creation. I would like to think that we are, right now, bringing it into being, but I do not believe any of us can completely envision where we are going. The best we can do now is create a vision of how we will come together as neighbors, God's children and inhabitants of creation, before it is too late.

Some contributors emphasize what I'll call an external model. I think Jim Deming sums this idea up well when he writes, "Your values are not your values until you act on them." These voices call for action: to challenge the status quo directly and fiercely. This means talking to your congregants, neighbors and Congress; it means questioning the media, our politicians and consumer culture; and it means getting your hands dirty. In these pages you have read a number of stories about small grassroots campaigns to change light bulbs, educate a congregation, or model sustainable behavior in the community that went well beyond anyone's original vision. Our places of worship, led by the voices in this book, are taking the moral lead for lifestyle change and they are getting things done, carried along by faith, fearlessness and usually not much money.

Meanwhile, others ask us to look first at our relationship to our Creator; our lives of worship and prayer must include care of creation – I'll call this an internal model. We cannot take up and sustain this enormous task of global mobilization, they advise, without a deep understanding of how our faith calls us to this challenge. It is not enough to change light bulbs, we must change our very hearts. These voices call us to look again at our sacred texts and scriptures, and see the truths that have been there all along: that our Earth is our home, our responsibility, a sacred place.

There's no real disagreement here, just a reflection of the fact that if we are going to change the world, we can only do it by going as deeply as we can in all the realms of our existence. We must change our hearts, reconnect our souls to the divine, and act on our new wisdom. We'll have to change a lot of old ideas and habits. The journey begins with the willing heart. Everyone in this book talks about the heart in one way or another, as the place where we find truth and where we connect with God and God's creation. Perhaps Pastor Clare Butterfield squares these visions most accurately when she says, "What we are trying to do is not to change light bulbs. We are trying to change people – with the assumption that they will then be the kind of people who will change their own light bulbs."

Along the way, we are encouraged to stay focused on the big picture and not get mired in little differences, or stuck in a state of despair or frustration. Both Rabbi Daniel Swartz and Dr. Joel Hunter, from very different spots on the religious spectrum, give us lessons in hope and conciliation. They know as well as anyone that this challenge will require humility, patience and a willingness to step out of our comfortable, self-referential worlds. But this is what our faith is about: We have the strength to keep moving forward. We are changing things, even if we can't always see the results of our labors.

It's going to be hard. Doing the right thing is seldom the easiest choice, but when it's apparent that this is the only choice for people of conscience, people of faith, we begin to heal. We will heal ourselves, our environment, and our planet. Who are we, as human beings, if not caretakers of creation? Stewardship of the planet and our care for one another is our greatest moral duty. The pursuit of justice, peace, health and harmony are our spiritual mandates. Who, if not our religious leaders, will show the way to this new creation? We can and we will love God and heal Earth.

# About Sally G. Bingham
# &
# The Contributors to
# *Love God, Heal Earth*

THE REV. CANON SALLY G. BINGHAM is a priest in the Episcopal Diocese of California, currently serving as the environmental minister at Grace Cathedral in San Francisco. She is the founder and executive director of The Regeneration Project, whose mission is to deepen the connection between ecology and faith. The Regeneration Project is primarily focused on a religious response to global warming through the Interfaith Power and Light Campaign, which has 26 state-affiliated programs and one in Washington, DC. A rapidly growing movement, IPL has 2000-plus member congregations representing more than 150,000 people. Projects based on the IPL model have been started by religious leaders as far away as Canada and Sweden. Active in environmental concerns for twenty years, Rev. Bingham serves on the national board of the Environmental Defense Fund, the advisory board of the Union of Concerned Scientists, the board of Environmental Working Group, and is the chair of the Diocese of California Commission for the Environment. Rev. Bingham's sermons often focus on the theological foundations for environmental stewardship, and can be heard live online at www.gracecathedral.org where she preaches on a regular basis. (www.theregenerationproject.org)

THE REV. WOODY BARTLETT is a retired Episcopal priest in the Atlanta Diocese. During his career he has had an active interest in involving the church in the world around it, and for the last twenty years he has focused this interest on the relationship between human beings and the creation. Rev. Bartlett is the author of *Living By Surprise: A Christian Response to the Ecological Crisis*. He is co-founder of Georgia Interfaith Power and Light and serves on its Steering Committee and Congregational Activities Committee. (www.gipl.org)

THE REV. DR. CLARE BUTTERFIELD is the director of Faith in Place, an interfaith environmental ministry in Chicago that gives religious people tools to become better stewards of creation. Faith in Place's over-400 Illinois congregations work together to support renewable energy, conserve energy, build markets for local sustainable agriculture and fair trade products, and train the next generation of stewards of the earth through urban agriculture with youth. Rev. Butterfield is an ordained Unitarian Universalist community minister. She has a J.D. from University of Illinois College of Law and a D.Min. from Chicago Theological Seminary, with a focus on faith and the environment. Illinois Interfaith Power and Light is a program of Faith in Place. (www.faithinplace.org)

MOHAMAD A. CHAKAKI holds a Masters Degree in Urban Ecology and Environmental Design from Yale University, and undergraduate degrees in religion and biology from George Washington University. His passion for nature and for people led him to work in parks and gardens across the U.S., with the Peace Corps in Central Africa, and the United Nations in Syria. He now consults environment and community development projects in both the US and the Middle East. Mohamad is part of a growing new network of "DC Green Muslims" that are active in environment and social justice issues in the Washington area. (www.dcgreenmuslims.blogspot.com)

THE REV. RICHARD CIZIK is the former Vice-President for Governmental Affairs of the National Association of Evangelicals and its 30 million members. His primary responsibilities included setting NAE's policy direction on issues before Congress, the White House and the Supreme Court, as well as serving as a national spokesman on issues of concern to evangelicals. Rev. Cizik is the author of over 100 published articles and editorials, and author and editor of *The High Cost of Indifference*. Called by the *New York Times* "The Earthy Evangelist" for his advocacy on climate change, he was on *Grist* magazine's list of "15 Green Religious Leaders." In 2008, Rev. Cizik was one of *Time* magazine's "100 Most Influential People."

RABBI ANDREA COHEN-KIENER is the director of the Inter-religious Eco-Justice Network, a faith-based initiative in environmental theology and practice, and is the spiritual leader of Congregation Pnai Or of Central Connecticut. She is the translator of *Conscious Community: A Guide to Inner Work* (Jason Aronson), by Rabbi Kalanymous Kalman Shapira, a rebbe in the Warsaw Ghetto. Andrea was ordained as a rabbi by the Alliance for Jewish Renewal. She is active in conflict resolution and political reconciliation, lecturing frequently on issues of ecology, spirituality and communication. A teen and family educator, she has written a manual for communication skills for teens, *Life on Earth: a User's Guide*. (www.irejn.org)

LINDA RUTH CUTTS served as Abbess and Senior Dharma Teacher of the San Francisco Zen Center from 2000 to 2007. A student of the revered Suzuki-roshi, she is a Soto Zen Buddhist priest now living at Green Gulch Farm Zen Center in Sausalito – having been one of the original small group that established it as a place of Buddhist practice and retreat in 1972. Her writings have been published in *Being Bodies: Buddhist Women on the Paradox of Embodiment* and *Buddhist Women on the Edge*, and in the Zen Center's journal *Wind Bell* and the Buddhist Peace Fellowship journal *Turning Wheel*. She serves on the Steering Committee of California Interfaith Power and Light. (www.sfzc.org)

THE REV. JIM DEMING is the executive director of Tennessee Interfaith Power and Light, working to bring earth stewardship and creation care to local congregations. He is also currently serving as the Interim Minister at First United Church in Nashville, TN. Jim holds an M. Div. from Emory University and an M. Ed. from Vanderbilt University. He has worked in religious publishing with Abingdon Press and Westminster/John Knox Press and served as a local church pastor in Ohio. He has been director of the Ohio Field Office for Rails-to-Trails Conservancy, director of the Tennessee Alliance for Legal Services (the state-wide support organization for legal aid), and director of the Kentucky/Tennessee Water Environment Association. (www.tn-ipl.org)

THE REV. DR. GERALD L. DURLEY has been the senior pastor of the historic Providence Missionary Baptist Church of Atlanta, Georgia, for the past 20 years, having earlier been a pulpit associate at Ebenezer Baptist Church in Atlanta. Active in the Civil Rights Movement of the 1960s, Rev. Durley holds a doctorate in Urban Education and Psychology from the University of Massachusetts and a Master of Divinity from Howard University, and is Adjunct Professor at Morehouse School of Medicine. Rev. Durley is deeply involved in global warming and climate change discussions across the country, working with scientists, clergy and environmentalists. He appears in the film *The Great Warming*. (www.providencemissionarybaptistchurch.org)

SR. PAULA GONZALEZ, SC, PH.D., futurist and environmentalist, is a Sister of Charity of Cincinnati. Formerly a professor of biology at the College of Mount St. Joseph, since 1975 she has offered over 1700 talks, seminars, mini-courses and retreats on various aspects of Planetary Awareness: "Learning from Earth," "Creating a Sustainable Future," "Renewable Energy," "Climate Change," "Ecospirituality," and "The Future of Religious Life." In the 1980s she gained direct experience with passive solar design by converting a chicken barn into a solar residence. A second major building project, also modeled on nature's cyclic processes, resulted in EarthConnection, a center for learning and reflection about "living lightly" on Earth. Sr. Paula has produced several book chapters, articles and audio and video programs. She is the co-founder of Ohio Interfaith Power and Light and serves on the steering team and the recently formed Board. (www.aea1.org/earthconnection.html)

THE REV. FLETCHER HARPER, an Episcopal priest, is executive director of GreenFaith, an interfaith environmental coalition based in New Jersey. An award-winning spiritual writer and nationally recognized preacher on the environment, he has developed a range of innovative programs to make GreenFaith one of the most respected religious-environmental groups in the US, finding ways for houses of worship and individuals to unite a love of God with a love of the environment. Prior to joining GreenFaith, Rev. Harper served as a parish priest for ten years and in leadership positions in the Episcopal Church. A graduate of Princeton University and Union Theological Seminary, he believes that caring for the Earth and revitalizing progressive religion are two of the greatest challenges facing the human family. (www.greenfaith.org)

DR. JOEL HUNTER is senior pastor of Northland, A Church Distributed, with 12,000 parishioners (and growing) at multiple locations in Florida and around the world (www.northlandchurch. net). An evangelical and an ordained United Methodist minister, Dr. Hunter is an energetic voice for conservative Christian environmental action and for broad cooperation and partnership — accomplishing more together than alone — as a way to achieve the greatest goals. Dr. Hunter serves on the board of the World Evangelical Alliance (420 million constituents) and the National Association of Evangelicals (30 million members) and has been featured in national publications and on the major television networks. He was on *Grist* magazine's list of the world's top 15 religious environmental leaders. His most recent book is *A New Kind of Conservative*. (www.northlandchurch.net)

LAUREL KEARNS is an associate professor of Sociology of Religion and Environmental Studies at Drew University's Theological School and Graduate Division of Religion, Madison, New Jersey. She is co-editor of *Ecospirit: Religions and Philosophies for the Earth* and a contributor to numerous books and journals on religion and ecological issues — with a particular focus on religious responses to global warming and the interplay of religions in social change. Professor Kearns serves on the board of GreenFaith, an interfaith environmental coalition in New Jersey, and is on the Steering

Committee of the Green Seminary Initiative, a movement designed to foster an ethic of ecological care for God's creation on seminary campuses. (www.webofcreation.org/greenseminary/index.htm)

REV. CHARLES MORRIS is a priest of the Catholic Archdiocese of Detroit and, since 1993, has served as pastor of St. Elizabeth Parish in Wyandotte, Michigan. St. Elizabeth has become well known for its innovative energy saving initiatives; it won the Energy Star® for Congregations award in 2001 and again in 2005. Rev. Morris founded Michigan Interfaith Power and Light in 2002, serving as its first director for five years. He is now MiIPL's director of public policy and public relations. MiIPL has over 200 member congregations, and is growing. Rev. Morris is active in the field of environmental justice. Besides having his work featured in the national media, he has published papers in peer-reviewed journals and at planning conferences. (www.miipl.org)

SR. PAT NAGLE, IHM is a member of the congregation of Sisters, Servants of the Immaculate Heart of Mary in Monroe, Michigan, and has ministered in a wide range of locales including the Midwest, Guatemala, California and the Pacific Northwest (her home). Her congregation's motherhouse undertook a major renovation project that was guided by their mission and by values of environmental stewardship. She is co-coordinator of Earth Home Ministries, a pioneering community-building, spirituality and sustainable living project that was featured in the video, *Ways We Live: Reclaiming Community*. In December 2007, she was a delegate with the World Council of Churches at the UN Convention on Climate Change in Bali, Indonesia. Presently she serves as co-chair of Oregon Interfaith Power and Light's Advisory Committee. (www.emoregon.org/power_light.php)

**BETH NORCROSS** helped launch the national Green Seminary Initiative (and currently serves as its Coordinator), and is a member of the steering committee for Greater Washington Interfaith Power and Light. She holds a master's degree in eco-theology from Wesley Theological Seminary and spearheaded Wesley's creation care and renewal program. She chairs the newly formed Wesley Creation Committee. Having enjoyed a long career in the environmental field, specializing in natural resources policy, Beth speaks and preaches on the Scriptural and ecological imperatives to protect the earth, and leads workshops and retreats on nature and spirituality. Her spirit/nature curricula include two for the National Council of Churches: "Sacred Waters," an adult education curriculum, and "Building a Firm Foundation," an eco-friendly building guide for churches. (www.webofcreation.org/GreenSeminary/index.htm)

**IMAM ACHMAT SALIE,** a native of South Africa, founded and directs the Islamic Studies program at Oakland University in Auburn Hills, Michigan. He is a board member of Michigan IPL and director of education, youth services, outreach and counseling at the Muslim Unity Center in Bloomfield Hills, Michigan. A passionate environmentalist, Imam Salie hopes to establish the first fully green Islamic community center. He counsels interfaith and interracial couples and speaks widely on topics of peace, ecology, gender equality, medical ethics and inter-religious tolerance. Imam Salie holds degrees in physics, biology, Arabic and Islamic Studies, and is completing his doctorate in business administration. (www.mulsimunitycenter.org)

**THE REV. FRED SMALL** is minister of First Church Unitarian, Littleton, Massachusetts, and co-chair of Religious Witness for the Earth (http://religiouswitness.org), a national interfaith network dedicated to public witness on critical environmental issues, especially global climate change. After graduating from Yale and the University of Michigan (J.D., M.S., Natural Resources), he worked as a staff attorney for the Conservation Law Foundation. Fred left the Foundation to tour internationally as a folksinger and songwriter, releasing seven albums over two decades (www.rounder. com). In 1999 he earned his M.Div. degree from Harvard. In July 2007, *Grist* magazine featured Rev. Small on its list of "15 Green Religious Leaders." (www.religiouswitness.org)

RABBI DANIEL J. SWARTZ is the spiritual leader of Temple Hesed (The Temple of Loving-Kindness), in Scranton, Pennsylvania, the city's oldest synagogue, founded in 1860. He recently completed two years as the coordinator for Greater Washington Interfaith Power and Light (GWIPL). Before that, Rabbi Swartz was executive director of the Children's Environmental Health Network, and served as associate director of the National Religious Partnership for the Environment. His published books include *To Till and To Tend: A Guide for Jewish Environmental Study* and *Action, and Faith Communities and Environmental Health: From Global to Local*, the latter winning the 2005 Award for Excellence from the Association of American Publishers. (www.gwipl.org)

MARY EVELYN TUCKER is a senior lecturer and senior scholar at Yale University, where she holds appointments in the School of Forestry and Environmental Studies, as well as the Divinity School and the Department of Religious Studies. She is co-founder and director of the Forum on Religion and Ecology and a research associate at the Harvard-Yenching Institute and the Reishcauer Institute of Japanese studies. Professor Tucker is the author of *Worldly Wonder: Religions Enter Their Ecological Phase*, and was the editor of

Thomas Berry's volume, *Evening Thoughts: Reflecting on the Earth as Sacred Community*. From 1997-2000 she served as a member of the Earth Charter Drafting Committee. (www.religionandecology.org)

THE REV. PAT WATKINS is an ordained minister in the Virginia Conference of the United Methodist Church, having served churches in the Lynchburg District. He and his wife, Denise Honeycutt, worked as missionaries in Nigeria with the United Methodist General Board of Global Ministries. He currently serves as the executive director of Virginia Interfaith Power and Light, and is a member of the United Methodist Women's Division Green Team for the denomination. Pat is an avid organic, permaculture gardener. He tries to live out his passion for God's creation by leading his life in such a way as to make a smaller footprint on God's earth – and to raise the awareness, particularly among people of faith, that there is a connection between faith and caring for creation. (www.vipl.org)

SR. GAIL WORCELO, a Passionist nun of St. Gabriel's Monastery, was given permission by her community in 1999 to begin a new monastery community, Green Mountain Monastery, with guidance from her longtime mentor, Passionist priest Fr. Thomas Berry, cosmologist and self-described geologian. Sr. Gail's particular focus has been the refounding of religious life in light of new understandings of the universe story. Through the founding of Green Mountain Monastery she hopes to contribute to bringing the Catholic religious tradition into its cosmological phase. Sr. Gail gives lectures and retreats on this theme, sharing her insights with groups throughout the United States and around the world. Sr. Gail is a liturgical dancer and choreographer, with degrees in clinical psychology and spirituality. (www.greenmountainmonastery.org)

# Acknowledgments

༄

I answered the phone in December 2007. The voice at the other end said, "Is this Sally Bingham?" "Yes," I said. " Have you thought about writing a book?" said the voice. " No, I have no time for writing. I am running a campaign. It is all I can do to keep up with the movement as it gains momentum." After some clever persuasion by my caller, I agreed to participate and the voice agreed to do most of the heavy lifting. Without Catherine Dees, my distinguished editor (the voice), our co-editor, Abby Dees, and my publisher, Paul Kelly, at St. Lynn's Press, there would be no book to record this amazing time in history, when mainstream religions embraced the call to address climate protection as THE moral issue of our time. And let there be no mistake. This book was their idea. Catherine has tirelessly labored with me and the others to produce a clear and focused understanding of the age in which we are living — an age of healing the earth with the intense involvement of diverse religious traditions. In the past, religion has played a major role in cultural changes. This movement is probably the most important one yet. It provides the hope and foundation for real, meaningful change.

Without the support of the creative group of people who agreed to write for this book, we couldn't have been able to give you the true picture of the movement. My heartfelt gratitude to all of you. Many are dear friends, but a few of you I know only by reputation. You are kind and generous with your time. I know, because time is one of our most precious commodities. Together we have produced a valuable piece of literature for both lay and clergy to wrestle with. From the personal stories to Scripture callings, the message is clear. We are on the forefront of a challenging movement in this country. One that will hopefully save creation before the damage is irreversible. Thank you all for helping to spread this message.

My friends from "before" who have supported and stuck with me from the moment I left the "former life" to do something more serious are very special, and without you I would not have been able to move with confidence. Jeanne Leonard, Johnny Drum and Jenepher Stowell, to name a few, but there are others. You have helped my ministry to flourish when others were doubtful.

And to my brother, Steve Grover, who has always held me in much higher esteem than I will ever deserve. I owe you, bro.

It would be neglectful not to mention the financial support from foundations and individuals, particularly The Regeneration Project's board of directors who have had the vision to recognize the value of the religious community being engaged in the dialogue about climate protection. The work would be impossible had you not taken the risk to help TRP get started. None of us knew the quick and immediate response would have been so rewarding. The rapid growth of the Interfaith Power and Light Campaign has surprised us all and simultaneously shown us that we are doing the right and moral thing.

Friends like Hunter Lovins, Steve Schneider, Karen Florini and Susan Stephenson who force me to see things as they really are, but also share their wisdom, have made my job at the helm of this ministry doable. And lastly, I want to mention Steve MacAusland who helped me to conceive the idea of Power and Light, "a religious response to global warming." His vision and courage at a time when people were still skeptical about human-induced climate change being real, is what inspired this movement. Our Episcopal Church held back, but he pushed me forward and said, "You are the one." Thank you, Steve.